Functional Awareness

Functional Awareness

Anatomy in Action for Dancers

Nancy Romita

AND

Allegra Romita

Oxford University Press is a department of the University of Oxford. It furthers
the University's objective of excellence in research, scholarship, and education
by publishing worldwide. Oxford is a registered trade mark of Oxford University
Press in the UK and certain other countries.

Published in the United States of America by Oxford University Press
198 Madison Avenue, New York, NY 10016, United States of America.

© Oxford University Press 2016

Library of Congress Cataloging-in-Publication Data
Names: Romita, Nancy, author. | Romita, Allegra, author.
Title: Functional awareness : anatomy in action for dancers / Nancy Romita and Allegra Romita.
Description: New York : Oxford University Press, 2016. | Includes bibliographical references and index.
Identifiers: LCCN 2015051067 | ISBN 9780190498139 (hardback)
Subjects: LCSH: Dance—Physiological aspects. | Dancers—Training of. | Mind and body. | Muscular sense. |
BISAC: MUSIC / Genres & Styles / Dance. | MUSIC / Genres & Styles / Ballet.
Classification: LCC RC1220.D35 R66 2016 | DDC 617.1/0275—dc23 LC record available at
http://lccn.loc.gov/2015051067
9780190498139 cloth
9780190498146 paper
9780190498153 updf
9780190498160 epub

Contents

Homage

Nancy and Allegra wish to pay homage to their somatic and embodied anatomy teachers, guides, and predecessors. It is by no means a complete list, but it identifies key influences in our current research.

Nancy owes gratitude to teacher/mentor Martha Myers and her visionary work to integrate somatic exploration with dance training at Nancy's alma mater, Connecticut College. In the 1970s Martha introduced Nancy to somatic work with Irene Dowd at Connecticut College as well as Bartenieff Fundamentals, Feldenkrais Method, Alexander Technique with Missy Vineyard, and Dance Movement Therapy with Linni Silberman and Elaine Siegel at the American Dance Festival. These early experiences in somatic education led Nancy on a lifelong exploration to support performing artists in discovering easeful use and integrated movement function. In addition, Nancy gives profound thanks to the American Center for the Alexander Technique, particularly her primary trainers, Judy Leibowitz, Barbara Kent, and Debbie Caplan, for providing a pathway to the psychophysical philosophies and principles she embodies and conveys daily through the work of FM Alexander. Alexander's approach to the relationship between structure, function, and use has deeply informed Nancy's somatic investigations.

Allegra pays homage to her coauthor and mother. She is a thoughtful and supportive parent, business partner, artist, mentor, friend, and somatic teacher. Allegra is grateful to her formative dance teachers at Towson University and University of Michigan. She thanks Sid McNairy, Amy Chavasse, and Ossi Raveh, who encouraged the yogi and the teacher within, and Ananda Apfelbaum for an approach to hands-on healing through Thai Massage Sacred Bodywork. She appreciates those who influenced her understanding of embodied anatomy: Amy Matthews, Marika Molnar, Khita Whyatt, Cheryl Clark, and John Chanik. In addition, Allegra is grateful to those who ignited her interest in dance education, writing, and curriculum design at NYU, particularly Dr. Susan Koff, Pat Cohen, Deborah Damast, and Claire Porter.

Both authors thank their predecessors in somatic literature, including FM Alexander, Irmgard Bartenieff, Mabel Todd, Margaret H'Doubler, Irene Dowd, Glenna Batson, Bonnie Bainbridge Cohen, Eric Franklin, Peggy Hackney, and Martha Eddy to name a few.

Finally, Nancy thanks her coauthor, collaborator, colleague, and daughter, Allegra. Her inspiring and innovative thinking on the relationship of biomechanical function and the artistry of movement is a gift. This journey is not possible without her partnership and coauthorship.

In the collective professional experience of training people in somatic-based practices, the authors have had vast and varied influences on their work. After many years of applying functional movement theory into practice, it is hard to distinguish the original sources of many of the practices and stories implemented. This book contains a bibliography to acknowledge the mentors, teachers, and literature that influenced this current path of integrated knowledge. If the authors are aware of the origin of a specific story or anatomical information, it will be referenced. There is a rich body of literature in embodied anatomy that precedes *Functional Awareness*. A suggested reading on each topic is provided at the end of the book to encourage readers to continue their investigations in embodied practices.

Acknowledgments

The authors thank the many people who supported this project by their generous gift of their time and talents. The authors owe a supreme debt of gratitude to Betsy Winship, our guide to editing and book publishing in the early stages of preparing the manuscript for submission. We thank Lisbeth Redfield, for her early belief, encouragement, and support for this book. We thank the anonymous readers for Oxford University Press. Their thoughtful comments helped shape and clarify our writing. Also we thank Norm Hirschy for his support and stewardship of the manuscript at Oxford University Press.

Many thanks to Jim Burger and JP Burger Photography for his artistic talents and photographs, Hollis McCracken for her pencil drawings, and Caitlin Duckwall for her artistic rendering of the FA® anatomical images.

In addition, we appreciate and thank Dr. Susan Kirchner at Towson University for encouraging us to deepen the research in somatic principles as they relate to the practice of dance performance. We thank Dana J. Martin, Wendy Salkind, and Jerri-Lynn Pilarski for their support as readers and generously contributing their thoughts and feedback.

Finally, both authors thank Vic Romita, loving husband and father, for his undying enthusiasm and support for all artistic endeavors partaken.

Introduction

Functional Awareness: Anatomy in Action for Dancers is an approach to understanding the body and how it functions through movement explorations in experiential anatomy with applications to dance training. It connects the scientific with the somatic. It connects anatomy with artistry. Applied practice of the Functional Awareness® principles enables one to efficiently recruit muscle actions to improve dance technique, release unnecessary muscular tension, and develop a balance between exertion and recuperation.

The book is a combination of two distinctive dance artists and their varied somatic backgrounds combining to form a connected process that stands as its own somatic approach. Allegra brings her background in Thai massage, yoga, dance performance for social change, movement science, and Laban Movement Analysis. Nancy's background in professional performance and choreography, Alexander Technique and functional anatomy adds additional perspectives to the development of this somatic approach. Together, over 35,000 hours of teaching, training, movement, and academic research supports the development of the principles in Functional Awareness®.

Similar to the tradition in modern dance where dancers are constantly inventing and reinventing new forms of movement expression, Functional Awareness® stands on the shoulders of the giants in embodied anatomy that precede us in order to integrate and create another lens on how humans move and how movement choices affect dance training and daily life.

Functional Awareness® is a movement philosophy based in the principles of efficient movement function, a lively curiosity to invite new body understanding, and a practice of nonjudgmental noticing, in order to appreciate the unique gifts in each dancing body. The reader is invited to apply the concepts in each chapter to dance skills as well as during quotidian or everyday tasks. Discovering daily mindfulness of body choices develops a profound deepening of one's dance artistry, while providing recuperation from the end-range actions of the rigorous requirements of dance.

This book is written for all dance enthusiasts interested in learning more about their body and offers tools to improve dance training. The book is for dancers, movement educators, professional dancers, and somatic practitioners. It is not an anatomy text, but rather a book introducing some anatomical concepts to provide cognitive context for sensory explorations. Basic principles of anatomy are discussed to enhance understanding of how the body can move with less stress and greater ease. The movement explorations and anatomical information establish a platform for exploration, discovery, and discussion. The material accumulates to create building blocks for mindful patterns in daily movement.

In dance we constantly seek the end-ranges of movement and often achieve spectacular artistic results. At times, it also results in a cost to our physical structure. It is our quest to develop strategies for stability and recovery, to discover efficiency of body action, and to provide simple, accessible tools so people can move for a lifetime with ease and grace.

Relationship of Habit to Dance Training

Functional Awareness® (FA) is a practical somatic method that provides a series of explorations in experiential anatomy to enhance our understanding of movement function, facilitate ease in body action, and improve dynamic alignment for dancing. FA investigates anatomical features of the skeletal structure, the muscular structure, and the myofascial tissue to help sustain elasticity, flexibility, and efficiency in movement, using the principles of release, recruit, and restore. *Functional Awareness: Anatomy in Action for Dancers* applies cognitive anatomical knowledge with a kinesthetic or sensory experience to deepen one's investigations to improve dynamic alignment and dance technique. It integrates anatomical theory, dance practice, and daily living, encouraging more choices of movement strategies. Most books on dance training seek to improve the dancer's actions in the training environment of the classroom. This book addresses studio practice and also presents mindful practices during daily life. These practices within daily life can have a profound impact on improving dance skills and provide tools to move with greater ease for a lifetime. Dance students using the FA training return after many years to express that the practices learned through this approach are still a part of their daily life, performing life, and teaching practice. This work seeks to create an embodiment of anatomy to facilitate ease and efficacy in movement.

Many people experience tension or pain and assume this is something that "just happens" to them. It is as if the body is a separate entity. People think of joint and body pain as being like a cold virus: we just pick it up from somewhere. Often there is no one particular event to precipitate the discomfort. Most muscular discomfort actually arises from something we do or more often it is the way in which we do it. If the action is repeated with frequency, it creates wear on the system and leads to pain and discomfort over time. In a sense, people "practice" discomfort through unconscious posture and movement habits. The following is an old joke to illustrate this point.

The Story: How Your Suit Fits

A woman has taken her pantsuit to be fixed and altered by a tailor. She tries on the outfit to be sure the alternations are correct. As she tries on the pants, she notices the leg lengths appear different.

The tailor is not interested in doing more work so he just adjusts her hip a bit and now the legs look even. The woman adjusts and decides she can live with this. The woman now tries on the jacket and discovers one sleeve is too long and also the darts make the jacket hard to button in the front. The tailor just says, "Look if you just make this little adjustment in your shoulders, it will fit perfectly."

The woman actually buys into this sales pitch, makes the adjustment, and walks out of the store. As she is walking out of the store and down the street two people are coming at her from the opposite direction. One says, "Look at that poor woman." "Yes," the other one says, "Doesn't her suit fit perfectly!"

People make subtle or larger adjustments in life and these adjustments become habits that are unconscious. Over time they begin to take a physical toll on our system. This toll is exhibited in tension, pain, stiffness, or rigidity of movement. The good news: It is possible to shift posture and movement habits and discover more ease and less tension in the body. Here are three simple approaches:

1. Become more aware of your personal movement habits.
2. Learn a basic understanding about how the musculoskeletal system functions, and how this affects body action.
3. Practice new skills to improve movement function and dynamic alignment.

Exploration: Becoming More Aware of Our Movement Habits

Try this experiment:

1. Clasp your hands together with all the fingers crossed.
2. Notice which thumb is on top. Is it your writing hand or your non-dominant hand?
3. Open your hands and close them quickly and unconsciously. Does the same arrangement in your thumbs and hand arise?
4. Now release your hands and reweave your fingers to place the other thumb on top. How comfortable or uncomfortable is this? Does it take a little more time for your brain to tell your body how to place your hands in this way?

Try the same activity with your arms crossed.

1. Fold your arms.
2. Notice which arm is on the top. Is this the same arm as the thumb earlier?

3. Drop your arms by your side and now raise your arms to fold the arms with the oppo-site forearm on top. How does this feel? Often we have a preferred manner in which we fold our arms and the other way feels a bit peculiar.

Try the same activity with legs crossed.

1. Cross your legs or your ankles if that is more familiar to you.
2. Notice which leg is on the top. Is this the same leg as the arm earlier?
3. Uncross the legs and then try the other side. How does this feel?

In facilitating this activity for over thirty years to thousands of people, we realize that these habits are not systemic and have no pattern in regard to dominant hand or genetic proclivity. They are merely "how your suit fits" or how you have made a habitual accommodation over time.

Some habits are compulsory and very positive, such as brushing our teeth or auto-matically moving the foot to the break pad when a light turns yellow and then red. Some habits are unnecessary.

Unconscious habits with posture can compromise body balance, place unnecessary stress on the system, and lead to discomfort and pain. Improving your range of choices for movement develops a more resilient neuromuscular system.

Your Findings and Why They Matter

My grandmother was born in 1900. Using life insurance statistics, the average life expec-tancy for a woman born in 1900 in America (married and a nonsmoker) was age fifty. Life expectancy for a woman born in 2000 who is married and does not smoke is now ninety!

We only get one skeletal system for a lifetime. If my grandmother had a little ar-thritis or chronic discomfort as she started to grow older, she had to deal with this only until age fifty (on average). We now live almost twice as long on average! It behooves us to know more about how our unconscious habits affect our musculoskeletal system and how this unconsciously contributes to chronic discomfort or worse. More importantly, we can prevent and change patterns of movement to alleviate pressure on the system through some techniques and practices in awareness.

Chronic unconscious misuse of the body leads to chronic discomfort or pain. A subtle habit can have a profound impact over time. Folding your hands does not have a large impact on your neuromuscular system, but crossing your arms often leads to many other accommodations so the body becomes imbalanced.

Crossing one leg far more often than the other can lead to an imbalance in the hips. If your legs are crossed right now, notice if you have more weight on one hip. You may want to check this out while you are driving. Are you always leaning slightly into one hip? This constant small imbalance creates instability in the lower back and pelvis, and this can lead to pain or discomfort over time. How you move through daily action affects your whole health.

The Anatomy: The Skeletal Structure

Our skeletal structure is the scaffolding that supports the other body systems. To have a framework of understanding about the body, it is helpful to be able to name and identify basic elements of the skeletal structure. (See Figure 1.1.)

There are seven vertebrae in the neck or cervical spine. The first cervical vertebra is called the atlas. Just as the Greek god Atlas held up the entire world, this first cervical vertebra holds up our world of ideas and thinking. The atlas or C1 vertebra articulates with the skull at the occiput. The top of our spine does not end at the base of the skull. The first vertebra or atlas meets the skull at the occiput. (See Figure1.2.)

The atlas is the pivot point to nod yes. If we begin the action at this place, minimal impact is made on the spine. If we habitually nod to look down at our computer or phone with the vertebra farther down the spine, the large muscle structures of the back have to do far more work. This can lead to muscle fatigue and pain.

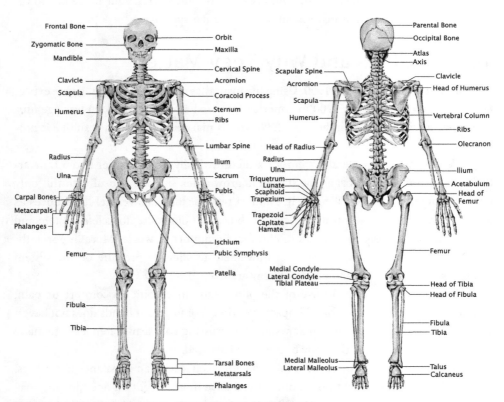

FIGURE 1.1 The skeletal system. (*Source/author*: Shutterstock)

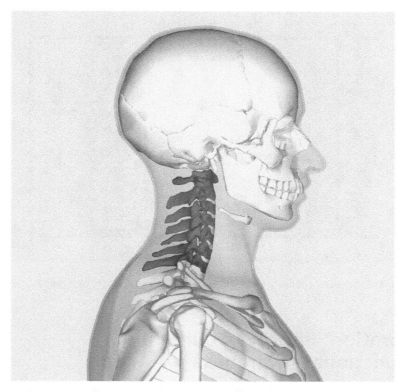

FIGURE 1.2 The skull and cervical spine. (*Source/author*: http://en.wikipedia.org/wiki/Cervical_ vertebrae#mediaviewer/File:Cervical_vertebrae_lateral2.png; *Gray's Anatomy* in the public domain)

Why Is This Structural Understanding of the Body Useful to Know?

Unconscious movement habits promote imbalance in the skeletal structure. It can be detrimental to the body, leading to pain and accelerated joint deterioration. How we stand or sit or hold our head affects overall function. Our head is the very top or most superior portion of the skeletal system. How it is poised on the spine has a very potent impact on how we move.

The adult head weighs ten to twelve pounds on average. How this structure is balanced at the top of our spine affects the rest of the musculoskeletal system in significant ways. The amount of physical exertion needed to support the head is minimal if it remains poised with the ears aligned over the shoulders and hips, as shown in the left image in Figure 1.3. If we have a habit of jutting our face forward to see the computer screen or to read this book, the amount of physical stress and energy can be up to three times greater on the system. This action to jut the face forward creates wear and tear on the vertebrae and fatigue and overuse symptoms in the muscle structure. This effect can be observed in the middle and right-hand images in Figure 1.3.

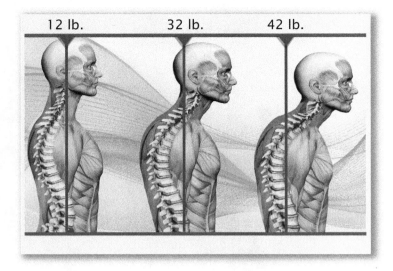

FIGURE 1.3 Habitual head posture's effect on the spine. (*Source/author*: With permission from Erik Dalton)

Exploration: Improve Your Skills for Functional Awareness® in Action

Notice the relationship of your head to your neck and spine in daily activities.

1. What happens to your neck and head when you slump, when you work at the computer? Does your head pull the face forward? This position actually tips the weight of the skull down onto the cervical vertebrae.
2. Do you like to bring your food up to your face, or do you bring your face to your food by pulling your face forward to the fork? This action of face forward compresses the cervical vertebrae.

How This Positioning Affects Dance Technique Training

In dynamic alignment, if your head is not aligned over the spine, this positioning creates instability. An example of how this can affect your dancing is a lack of reliability for a clear turning axis. It is harder to balance and it is more difficult to execute multiple turns reliably. Your ability for vertical height in jumping is compromised as well. It is very difficult for the body to suddenly align the head during a dance phrase if most of the day you are craning the head forward while looking at your cell phone or computer screen.

Suggestions for Daily Practice to Facilitate a Shift in Habit and Improve Dance Skills

For all daily practices, follow a simple three-step process:

1. Discover how your "suit fits." What are your habits for head balance, arm cross, and leg cross? None of this is wrong or bad posture. It is merely an unconscious pattern that can contribute to imbalance in the system. We all have habits of asymmetry. It is awareness of these habits and choosing when they are necessary that enhances postural health and efficiency of movement.
2. Consider letting yourself move out of habit and into a state of curiosity about balancing the body differently. Play with letting your eyes gaze the horizon to rebalance where the first vertebra of the atlas meets the skull or occiput (the AO joint).
3. Keep a movement journal to record your findings. This journal can help you notice patterns over time.

Skeletal Center of Gravity

Moving out of Habit and into a Balanced Standing Posture

Standing is a daily activity that can promote balance, or it can systemically compromise the spine and be a source for discomfort and pain. Habit plays an important role in the choices one makes for standing. The principles for easeful standing involve moving toward symmetry in the body. No one is completely symmetrical. It is important to move the body toward symmetry and balance so you exert equal force on your structure. Unequal force over time compromises the body structure and weakens joints and muscles.

The Story: *My Three Sons*

One student, John, a tall gentleman in his late forties, came to see me because he had severe and chronic back pain in his lower back or lumbar area. He had tried surgery involving spinal fusion. This surgery provided a temporary relief, but over time his pain returned.

Figure 2.1 shows what John's posture looked like.

I explained to John that, as young babies and toddlers, our standing balance is well organized with little unnecessary effort. Over time we start to accommodate to our surrounding environment. For example, tall people may slouch down to accommodate to a chair that is too small. As people move into the teenage years there are psychophysical accommodations that are often made unconsciously. A teenager may think that he is too tall and intentionally slouch. Someone else may feel too short and try to lift his chin to appear taller.

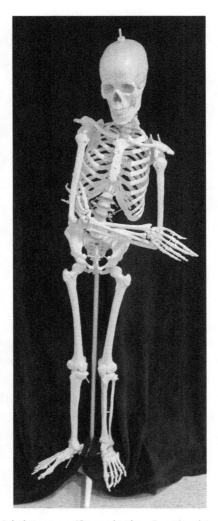

FIGURE 2.1 John's posture. (*Source/author*: Functional Awareness®)

During this explanation to John, he exclaims, "Oh! I know where this habit of standing comes from! When I was a boy there was a TV show called My Three Sons, *and at the start of every show they had the three sons standing there with one son tapping his foot during the theme song. The teenage boy, Rob, was so cool on that show. I remember when I was ten, I said to myself 'I am going to be cool and stand like Rob'!"*

Most people do not have an "aha" moment as to when they begin to take on a habit. People do have the capacity to observe current patterns and begin to think consciously about how our environment does affect stance in life. When the brain thinks about the principles of balance, the body's muscle system responds. Using the tools of Functional Awareness®, John was able to shift his postural habits, relieve his chronic back pain, and feel in more control of his body actions.

Exploration: How Does Your Suit Fit While Standing?

There are two key habits to observe in standing. How are your feet connecting to the earth? Where is your head in relation to the rest of your spine? Try the following experiment:

1. Close your eyes while facing a mirror. Stand for a moment as if you were waiting in line at the grocery store. Just settle into the habit that feels comfortable in standing.
2. Open your eyes. Notice if you are standing on leg more than the other.
3. Notice if one foot is farther out ahead than the other.
4. Place your palms on your hips and notice if one hip bone is rotated forward.
5. Now stand with a side view to the mirror and close your eyes to find your habit in standing.
6. Open yours to eyes. Are your head and face forward of the rest of your spine?
7. Are you leaning forward on the balls of your feet or back on your heels?

Your Findings and Why They Matter

Answer these questions for yourself:

1. While dancing, do you favor using one leg to turn over the other?
2. Do you have one leg that you prefer as your standing leg? For example, does one leg support you in adagio movement more reliably?
3. Do you prefer fifth position with the right leg in front? Or how about the left leg in front? Do these feel the same?

Recognizing your standing habit is the gateway to understanding movement efficiency in dance. It is a bit easier to observe habitual idiosyncrasies while standing still. If you wear out your left shoe more than your right shoe, this indicates that you habitually place more weight on that foot as well as that hip, creating a pattern to "wear out" that side of your body at a faster rate than the other side. You can prevent this with a simple reminder to move toward balanced standing.

The Anatomy: Skeletal Center of Gravity

Your skeletal system can balance in standing with minimal stress to the neuromuscular system. Unconscious habits of imbalance cause chronic strain that lead to discomfort and pain.

If you are standing with your center of gravity (COG) aligned, as shown in Figure 2.2, the body musculature is balanced and there is little stress on the system.

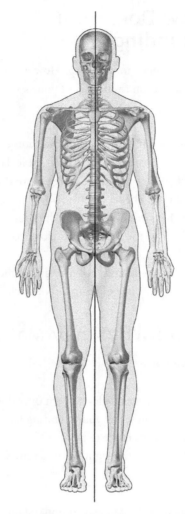

FIGURE 2.2 Skeleton COG front view. (*Source/author*: Functional Awareness® and Caitlin Duckwall)

Many people are like John and develop unconscious poor posture habits, moving the center of gravity into imbalance. When the system is not balanced through the COG, muscles overwork and uneven skeletal alignment places unnecessary pressure on the vertebrae and joints.

Look at the line down the middle in the front view of the skeleton depicted in Figure 2.2. This line is often referred to as the plumb line of balance for the body in the sagittal plane. The mid-sagittal plane equally divides the body into right and left halves. If you stand in the "cool Rob" from *My Three Sons* position, throwing the weight into one hip more than the other, you create an imbalance in the neuromuscular system.

Look at the person in balanced standing on the grid in Figure 2.3. The line identifying the frontal or coronal plane separates the body into front and back halves. If the face

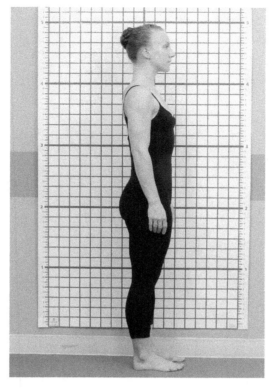

FIGURE 2.3 Balanced standing. (*Source/author*: With permission from Jim Burger Photography)

juts forward, as mentioned in the previous chapter, the COG moves, creating an imbalance in the neuromuscular system that can lead to muscle fatigue and discomfort. If your weight is falling back on your heels, the rest of your system starts to "'grab'" or hold on to muscle tension to prevent you from falling backward. Leaning too far forward on the balls of the feet or too far back on the heels can be common causes for back pain. If you are leaning forward with more weight on the balls of your feet, so the COG line falls through your kneecaps (patella), unnecessary pressure is placed on the pelvis, hips, and particularly knees.

Importance of the Balance at Your Feet

Where your balance is at your feet is important to discover in order to maintain dynamic alignment. Many people think of the foot as one lump that fits into a shoe. The foot is actually composed of twenty-six articulating bones. In addition, the foot contains a couple of sesamoid bones (bones embedded in tendons) to provide shock absorption or cushion for the ball of the foot. With twenty-six articulating bones and thirty-one joints, we have many choices for how we stand on our feet.

Easeful balance is often achieved if the foot is resting evenly at three points of contact. These points of contact are called the tripod of balance. Anatomically speaking, these

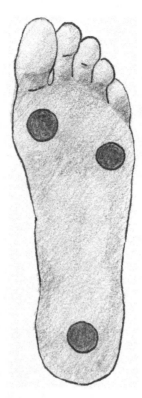

FIGURE 2.4 Tripod of the foot. (*Source/Artist*: With permission from Hollis McCracken)

balance points are the distal head of distal first metatarsal, the distal head of the fifth meta-tarsal, and the anterior calcaneus or between the lateral and medial malleoli. Figure 2.4 helps to visualize these points of balance on the bottom of the foot. If the feet are balanced and the head is poised through the COG (demonstrated in Figure 2.3), the body often "corrects" many posture imbalances unconsciously when the key points for balance at the feet and the head are well organized.

Exploration: Getting out of Habit for the Feet

This simple exploration applies gentle pressure to the soles of the feet. In this way the habitual stance for balance becomes unhabituated. It then releases habitual tension and allows the foot to discover the tripod of balance with ease.

Part 1
1. Take one or two athletic socks and roll them up in a ball.
2. Stand with your feet in parallel, with equal weight on both feet. The feet about hip distance apart.

3. Place the sock under the right foot so it is about center on the arch.
4. Now move both feet forward onto your toes and lift the heels off the floor. Then rock back onto the heels, rolling gently through the pressure of the sock. Repeat this several times.
5. Take the sock out from under the right foot. See if the right foot feels different from the left. For some it may feel odd, for others it may feel more stable, and for some it does not feel very different. All these experiences are valid and helpful in terms of letting the body move out of habit and into awareness.

Part 2
1. Repeat Steps 1 to 5 with the sock under the left foot.
2. Notice if there is a change.

Here are some other helpful guidelines to easeful balance in standing:

1. Place your feet equally on the three points of contact called the tripod of balance.
2. Let your eyes gaze at a point on the horizon because this often helps to balance the head at the atlanto-occipital joint mentioned in the first chapter.
3. Align your ears, shoulders, hips, and ankles while standing.

Mindfulness in Dance Class

1. When you are watching the teacher demonstrate an exercise, notice your habitual patterns for standing. Are you leaning into a hip? Is it almost always the same hip? Is one foot always out ahead of the other with the hip also rotated forward? These habits cause muscular imbalances that make dynamic alignment more difficult during the actual exercises of dance practice and performance.
2. If you notice one foot ahead of the other or more weight on one leg, practice the following: pause and allow for a breath, gently shift the feet to discover the tripod of balance, let your focus gaze out at eye level, and let the rest sort itself out. It is not about attaining a position; it is about making a choice to move in the direction of balance.

Over the years students have asked for some helpful information on how to stand for long periods of time, as the body seeks a balanced reciprocity between exertion and recuperation. To prevent fatigue the body appreciates small, frequent adjustments to maintain a dynamic alignment.

Tips for Standing for Long Periods of Time

1. Let your eyes focus out to the horizon to let your head poise on your spine and find the tripod of balance for your feet.

2. Gently shift your weight through the tripod by subtly moving toward the right front big toe, and then to the outside of the foot, moving back to the weight on the right heel. Then shift the weight to the left heel and around to the outside of the left foot and onto the big toe of the left foot. This slow, gentle, circular shift of weight ensures a lively dialogue between your body habit for standing and dynamic alignment.

Mindfulness in Daily Life

1. When you are waiting in a line at the grocery store, notice your habitual patterns for standing.
2. Pause and allow for a breath. Let your eyes gaze the horizon. Discover the tripod of balance at your feet, and let the rest sort itself out.

Gentle reminder: There is no wrong way to stand. The body can move in many ways. You are merely considering the role that unconscious habit has in contributing to imbalances in your structure and making some choices to recuperate from those stresses by moving out of habit and into awareness.

Anatomical and Kinesthetic Imagery

Impact of Thinking on Doing

Imagery to improve dance function has an illustrious lineage. Mabel Todd, a pioneer in kinesthetic anatomy, wrote an innovative book in 1937, entitled *The Thinking Body*. Her work is important to note in relation to somatic work and dance training. Lulu Sweigard worked with Todd and developed studies in ideokinetic imagery. Irene Dowd followed with her inspiring book, entitled *Taking Root to Fly*. In 1926 Todd studied body alignment and patterns of coordination. The work of Mabel Todd, linked with other somatic models, inspired a new approach to the education of dance deeply rooted in imagery. These innovative philosophies on teaching dance were integrative, linking the domain of the intellect with the realm of the body.

As founder of University of Wisconsin's dance program in 1926, Margaret H'Doubler professed the philosophy that "[dance] technique must be experienced in a way that recognizes the anatomical, physiological, and psychological connections and disciplines" (1998, p. 96). This somatic-based philosophy on dance education inspired Nancy Topf during her study with H'Doubler at Wisconsin. Nancy Topf's repatterning technique works with kinesthetic imagery as a tool for alignment, awareness, and exploration of movement vocabulary (Cho, 1998; Dixon, 2005). Currently Eric Franklin is a prolific writer of the twenty-first century, providing strategies for using imagery to dance technique. These somatic pioneers, among others, have influenced dance teachers to aid students toward improved performance and body understanding through imagery.

Recent research substantiates the premise that just thinking about something changes skeletal and muscular response in the body. A sample of the current research can be found at http://www.nytimes.com/2010/02/02/science/02angier.html?pagewanted=all&_r=0.

Thinking has a pivotal relationship to dynamic alignment and balance.

The Story: Chips the Dog with Ballon

In a modern technique class offered at Towson University's Burdick Hall, my students and I decided to try this informal experiment. The students were performing jumps at the barre. One student informally measured the height of the jump of her partner, using the lines provided by the cinderblock wall next to the barre as a reference point. Next I told the following story about Chips the dog.

On Sundays we would drive to my in-law's house outside New York City for a delicious meal of pasta with a red meat sauce. They had a miniature beagle named Chips. Each week we walked up to the front door and rang the doorbell. Chips would scurry to the door, barking. The door was solid on the bottom but had a window on the top portion. Chips jumped to try to see who it was. She would jump and jump and jump effortlessly, ears flying up, for minutes until someone unlocked the door (see Figure 3.1).

Chips had what is called ballon *in ballet technique, the appearance of lightness while jumping. The students imagined Chips and then repeated the jumps while continuing to think of the image of Chips and her head and ears flying up as they performed a few easy jumps. The students returned back to the barre and repeated the jumping exercise while the partner observed. Each student demonstrated a quantitative, measurable improvement in the height of the jumps.*

The use of imagery is a powerful teaching tool. Thinking can have a profound effect on the body to elicit or prevent improvement in dance skills. As mentioned in the first chapter, unconscious habits can also inhibit improvement. Changing your thinking can change your dancing.

Exploration: Thinking Up and Thinking Down

1. In pairs or on your own: Partner A stands in front of Partner B. Partner A closes her eyes and imagines her whole body filling with heavy wet cement from the top of the head to the feet. Take your time to sense that cement weighing down each structure of the body so the head sits heavily on the neck and the ribs sink under the weight of

FIGURE 3.1 Chips jumping. (*Source/Artist*: With permission from Hollis McCracken)

the cement onto the pelvis and the pelvis sits on the legs. Let the cement spill out your feet and fill the room so you are in cement up to your ankles . . . and then the cement hardens. Partner B gently tries to lift Partner A off the floor. If you are exploring this on your own, then try jumping a few times while maintaining the image of the cement.

2. Now Partner A imagines that her head is a hot-air balloon and the side body is like the strings and the pelvis is the basket on the balloon. At first the feet are sandbags holding it down (gravity's pull), and then imagine lift off. Partner B lifts Partner A. Again if you are experimenting with this on your own, just try a few jumps.

3. Consider these differences with your partner or consider these differences for yourself.

4. Repeat with the other person in front so each has a turn to "think up" and "think down."

Your Findings and Why They Matter

When thinking up, you are employing the deep postural support system and the body moves with more ease and efficiency. When you are thinking down, you are over-recruiting large muscle groups to engage unnecessarily and the action becomes much harder as the body ends up working its natural tendencies for poise and balance. One of the primary places to recognize unnecessary pressure down on the spine and an increased sense of weight is at the top of spine, where the first vertebra, called the atlas, meets the skull at the occiput.

The Anatomy: Clarification of the Atlanto-occipital Joint to Provide a Framework for Anatomical Imagery for "Up"

The skull has a large hole (the foramen magnum) where the spinal cord travels from the skull and the vertebrae for the spinal column for the spinal cord to disseminate nerve function through the rest of the body (see Figure 3.2). The first cervical vertebra (the atlas) articulates at the occiput to form the atlanto-occipital joint, often referred to as the AO joint (Figure 3.3). If the head is tipped back, it places pressure on the AO joint and the rest of the spine. If the face is pulled forward with eyes down, as one often does while using a cell phone, this posture also causes unnecessary stress on the spine. It is simple to discover the correct poise of this joint and to find your natural upright balance in the body. Try the following movement exploration.

Exploration: Discover Integrity of Balance at the Atlanto-occipital Joint

1. Place one finger just under the flesh behind the chin (just superior to the hyoid bone) and one at the nuchal notch at occipital ridge or base of the skull.

2. Pull the face forward to look out at this page.

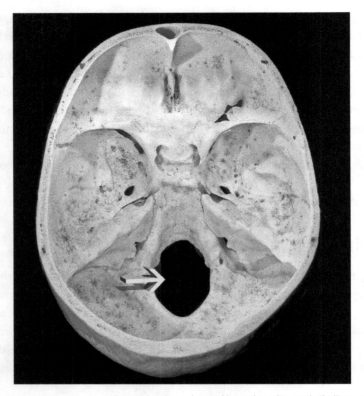

FIGURE 3.2 Foramen magnum. (*Source/author*: https://en.wikipedia.org/wiki/Foramen_magnum [public domain]; http://creativecommons.org/licenses/by-sa/3.0/)

3. Notice what happens at the base of the skull. Pull the chin and neck back into "straight posture" that we as dancers often think is needed to align the spine. Sense the front of the neck and jaw. The skull is actually pressing down on the spine in both of these movements, so the head feels heavy and there is more tension in the muscles of the neck.

4. Explore a balance between the head and neck where the head feels easeful and poised to balance. This balance requires less effort and feels more relaxed.

The above exercise was inspired by the work of Judy Leibowitz while she was teaching at The Juilliard School (see Further Readings).

Your Findings and Why They Matter

Once the AO joint is balanced, the deep muscles of the spine can support the body with ease. Chips the dog displayed this beautiful dynamic alignment each week as she jumped at the front door. For dancers these deep muscles and the poise of the head provide strong integrity for the complicated actions needed to jump, turn, or balance on one leg. If the AO joint is compressed, the rest of the body responds with tension.

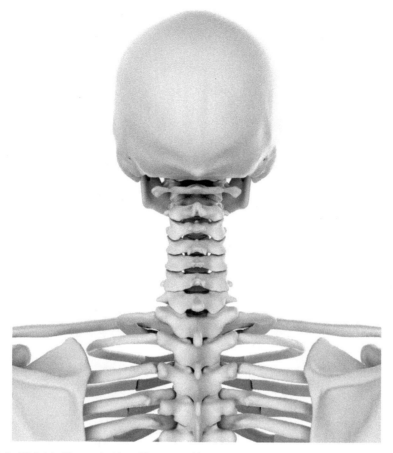

FIGURE 3.3 AO joint. (*Source/author*: Shutterstock)

Mindfulness in Dance Class

Notice if your chin likes to lift up as you prepare for a turn or jump. See if you can reassess this, release unnecessary tension, and balance the AO joint to allow for efficient muscle recruitment. If you spend most of your day with your AO joint in imbalance, it is difficult to discover this balance easily when you are preparing to balance or turn.

Think about Chips' ears flying up as you practice jumps during class. Or just think "up" so the head leads the movement into the air rather than pushing up from your feet.

Mindfulness in Daily Life

When walking from a car or train into work, or from your dorm to class, take a moment to "think down" and see how that affects how your body feels. No need to judge the sensation, just notice. Now "think up" and see what happens.

Deep Muscles of Postural Support

When we are infants and toddlers, we naturally balance the head and sit and stand with a lengthened spine. As we get older unconscious habits interfere with this natural balance. One does not have to grip to stand up or work hard to sit up straight. The body has an inherent system of balance.

For people to regain this natural poise, it helps to first think or imagine the skeletal structure in order for the muscular system to act efficiently. If the skeletal structure is balanced through the center of gravity (COG), the postural muscles will activate. The pull-down from gravity elicits the response for the muscles to suspend the skeletal system upright with ease. If the head is pulled forward off the COG or there is an imbalance at the feet, the body exhibits a lack of efficiency in motion and muscular overuse occurs.

The Story: Discovering Gravity's Effect on Posture

In the 1960s, NASA scientists were focused on the space race to the moon. During the Apollo missions with three astronauts in the capsule, the astronauts were in a weightless environment for longer and longer periods of time. The astronauts would "splash down" to Earth by landing in the ocean. The astronauts were carried out in huge cargo nets onto the ship. Once on board, it became apparent that they could not stand! It took up to a week for some of them to regain standing balance. This led the support team to think there was muscle atrophy in space, so they designed ways for the astronauts to maintain large group muscle function through resistance training. The astronauts prepared for the next mission, flew into space and returned, but still could not stand up for days after the return from the weightless environment in the space capsule. The team realized that a group of postural support muscles very close along the spine are autonomic. These muscles lengthen the spine and support the body in upright posture every day as a natural "righting system" for balanced movement. They contain slow twitch or Type 1 muscle fibers, rich in mitochondria, which enable them to function constantly and effortlessly for long periods of time, but they require a trigger. This trigger is gravity. When gravity pulls down, these muscles then engage to lengthen and support the body in upright posture. Standing and dancing is the delicate relationship with gravity and energy. Hence, gravity is not a force weighing us down; it is the impulse for us to stand up!

The Anatomy: Type 1 Muscles of Postural Support

The deep postural muscles help us interact with gravity in a resilient fashion. If we interfere with these deep stabilizing muscles, the much larger muscles of the back begin to execute the muscular effort required. One can perform the task of upright posture with the larger, more superficial muscles, but this requires more effort, uses much more energy, and the muscles become fatigued more quickly. The body experiences this fatigue as tension or pain.

The muscles illustrated in Figure 4.1 are known collectively as the suboccipital muscles. These muscles are predominantly local stabilizers. If the skeletal system is in balance, they can work autonomically and tirelessly to maintain balance of the head and neck.

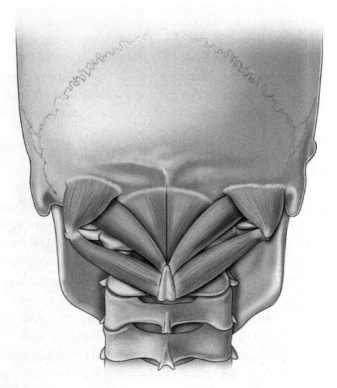

FIGURE 4.1 Suboccipital muscles. (Functional Awareness® and artist Caitlin Duckwall)

Figure 4.1 illustrates the four specific muscles of the suboccipitals: the rectus capitis posterior major and minor and the obliquus capitis superior and inferior. They are short muscles with limited mobility. They aid in extension, side bending of the cervical spine, and limited rotation at C1 and C2 (nodding yes and no). These muscles function constantly and subconsciously to maintain spinal balance while we are sitting, standing, walking, and dancing. They are primarily what are called Type 1 or stabilizing muscle fibers.

In addition to the suboccipital muscles, another primary Type 1 muscle group for postural support is the transversospinalis. The transversospinalis group is comprised of three sets of muscles that are very deep along the spine and run superomedially from transverse process to spinous process. The rotatores span one vertebra and are closest to the spine. The multifidus muscles span three vertebral levels and lie just superficial to the rotatores. The semispinalis is the most superficial muscle and spans five or six vertebral levels. These muscles aid extension, flexion, and rotation, depending on their responses to other muscles, but they are pivotally important for upright posture. Together they form a strong "braid" or chevron along the spine to allow for spinal mobility and postural stability (Figure 4.2).

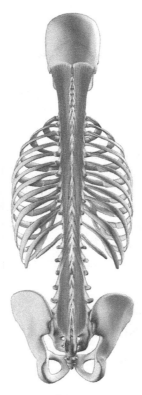

FIGURE 4.2 Transversospinalis muscle group. (*Source/author*: Functional Awareness® and artist Caitlin Duckwall)

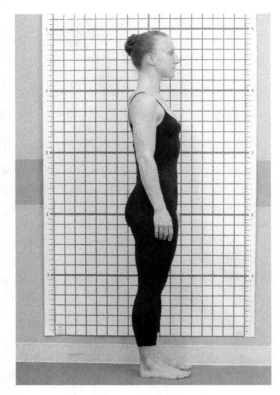

FIGURE 4.3 Points of balance. (*Source/author*: With permission from Jim Burger Photography)

Understanding the inherent muscle structure to support a lengthening spine is useful to discovering efficiency of movement and freedom from unnecessary effort and tension. As dancers, we often think that demonstrating effort and tension is a good thing, but unnecessary effort impedes expressivity.

If the body is balanced through the COG (Figure 4.3), the Type 1 muscles of the transversospinalis fire easily, tirelessly, and without pain. The pull downward from gravity elicits the response for the muscles to suspend the skeletal system upright with ease. You were experiencing this ease of motion in the first movement exploration in Chapter 3, called "thinking up and thinking down." Gravity, pulling us to the earth, provides a trigger for these muscles to activate and sustain us in dynamic alignment.

Exploration: Kinesthetic Sensing of the Transversospinalis Muscles

Put your arms at your side and hands resting with the third finger facing your leg at the side seams of your pants. Take a moment to envision the poise of the head, the balance at the tripod of your feet, and the plumb line of balance through the ears, shoulders, hips, and ankles.

Stretch and extend your fingers toward the ground to enhance the pull of gravity and then "think up" to engage the transversospinalis. You will often feel a sensation of the spine lengthening energetically. If you have a partner, let your partner tug at the fingers to enhance this sensation. If you are on your own, you can use small free weights.

Your Findings and Why They Matter

When thinking up, you are employing the deep postural support system and the body moves with more ease and efficiency. When you are thinking down, you are over-recruiting large muscle groups to engage unnecessarily and the action becomes much harder as the body ends up working its natural tendencies for balance.

Mindfulness in Dance Class

Many exercises in dance training begin with a musical preparation. During these moments of preparation, think of pressing the tripod on your feet into the floor and "think up" through your whole spine. Do not "pull" for up. The body and transversospinalis will engage to naturally lengthen with your thinking.

Mindfulness in Daily Life

When carrying grocery bags from the store, distribute the weight of the bags evenly between your two hands. As practiced in the movement exploration above, "think up" as the weight of the bags pull down. This counterbalance between gravity and energy improves dynamic alignment and whole health for your back.

Motions of the Trunk and Elegant Use of Spiral

The balance of upright posture is an excellent place to begin the discoveries in ease of movement, but the body moves in a myriad of wonderful ways to satisfy a required skill or activity. Dancers train to be adaptable to many movements with varied tempos and phrasing. It is possible to enrich this training through skeletal and muscular awareness. Sensing a connection from the head through the pelvis to the feet facilitates a primary organization to allow spirals, twists, and innovative creative movements to unfold. There are tremendous benefits in exploring somatics-based dance training and embodied anatomy to enhance movement potential in the spiral motions of the spine.

The Story: Dancing for a Lifetime

It was a warm summer evening in New England. We were in a black box theater at Dean College in Franklin, Massachusetts. At seventy-five years old, master dancer, choreographer, educator, and performer Bill Evans performed not just one but two solo works on the program. When onstage, his body exudes a litheness that belies his years. He moves through the space with a connectivity and expressivity that draws you in to the smallest gesture and surprises you when the movement darts through space (see Figure 5.1).

He embodies the resiliency and elasticity inherent in the spiral nature of our neuromuscular system and transforms the movement from "steps" into art. He has been performing since he was nine. During much of his career, he has been in a deep practice of embodied anatomy and somatics-based dancing. His practice inhibits limitation and permits possibility.

The body is not composed of straight lines and right angles. It is an elegant design of curves and spirals to provide resilient strength. The resilient nature of the spine and the supporting muscular and myofascial system is a wonderful spiral web to provide choices in movement. Dance master Bill Evans embodies the inherent design of the possible

FIGURE 5.1 William (Bill) Evans. Photo credit: Jim Dusen

movements in the trunk. Exploring movement activities along with anatomical information enhances the awareness of body functioning, and the body can release habitual holding to develop increased flexibility and strength. The following exploration reveals information about one's individual spinal flexibility.

Exploration: Discovery of Spinal Preferences

A. Spinal Roll Down from the Wall: Flexion and Extension
   1. Lean with your back against the wall and your heels 4 inches away from the wall. Place your feet a comfortable distance apart and in parallel, and begin to roll down. Instead of rolling down by moving away from the wall, try pressing each vertebra or part of the spine into the wall and then roll down bringing your head toward the floor. The effect feels like the inside of a wave as it crests. This movement allows the body to sense the spine and where it articulates easily with the wall and where it moves in chunks away from the wall.

2. Gently bend the knees and keep them slightly bent as you roll back up the wall, seeing if you can feel the vertebrae connecting back to the wall.

3. Repeat Steps 1 and 2 one more time.

4. See if you notice any difference in your overall contact with the wall and in your dynamic elasticity of the back.

5. Now step away from the wall completely. Perform a spinal roll down without the wall for support. See if this spinal articulation is now different from your habitual manner of rolling forward.

B. Side Bending Right and Left: Lateral Flexion

1. Once again along the wall, with the legs in a wide second position and arms overhead in a wide V, how far can you bend to the side? Can you bend the same amount to the other side?

2. Does the sensation of stretch on the side of your body feel equal on both sides?

C. Spiraling to the Right and Left: Spinal Rotation Right and Rotation Left

1. Step away from the wall and place your feet in a wide parallel position. Consider the tripod of balance at the feet and the balance of the head.

2. Close your eyes and turn your head and spine to the right, letting the arms wrap around your torso.

3. Open your eyes and see how far you have turned.

4. Now repeat to the other side. Is it easier to turn your head and spine one direction than the other?

Your Findings and Why They Matter

Daily habits can affect our ability to twist, turn, and maintain flexibility for dance performance. Habit can create stiffness and lack of mobility in specific areas of the spine and torso over time. For example, if you always sleep with your head turned to one side, these many hours in one position create a flexibility to turn to that side and develop a restriction of movement on the other side over time. If you always tuck one knee up tight to your chest when sleeping, this position creates an imbalance in the pelvis and sacroiliac joint and muscular imbalances in the back and also the deep psoas muscle of anterior postural and pelvic support. The imbalanced rotation for long periods of time during sleep has an affect on the ability to turn more efficiently in one direction more than the other direction. Understanding the anatomy is a key to understanding body patterns.

The Anatomy: Spinal Curves

The spine has several sections and each one has a slight curve that provides a resiliency in the structure for adaptive movement. The cervical, thoracic, lumbar, and sacral sections contain curves that support the range of movement of the torso. The seven bones of the

neck are called cervical vertebrae, as discussed in Chapter 1. The twelve thoracic vertebrae each have costal bones or ribs that are attached to their transverse processes. The five
lumbar vertebrae connect the ribs to the pelvis, and the five fused bones of the sacrum
create the end of the spine with the one to three fused bones of the coccyx comprising
the inferior tip. When viewed from the side the spinal column has four curves. The cervical spine curves slightly inward. The thoracic spine curves slightly outward. In the lower
portion, the lumbar spine curves inward with the sacrum slightly outward. The curves
provide a range of motion between flexion and extension in the torso. People can display
some imbalances in the spinal curvature as illustrated in Figure 5.2.

Lordosis (swayback) is the shape of the spine in the lower back. Doctors use the
term hyperlordosis for curves that are greater than usual. The term kyphosis is used to
describe the thoracic spinal curve that results in a hunched or rounded back. Scoliosis is
an abnormal lateral curvature of the spine. In scoliosis the spine curves to the side, and
each vertebra also rotates on the next one in a corkscrew fashion.

If one section of the spine has excessive curvature, the balance of resiliency is upset
and the body develops patterns of overuse and tension. In some cases these curves are
a genetic feature and passed down through families. This condition is called idiopathic

(a)

FIGURE 5.2 (A) Lordosis, (B) kyphosis, and (C) scoliosis. (*Source/author*: With permission from Jim
Burger Photography)

(b)

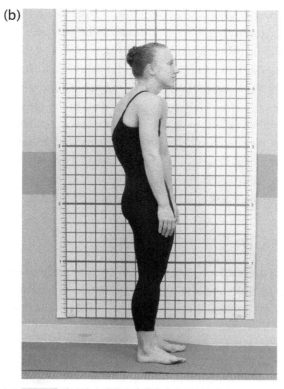

(c)

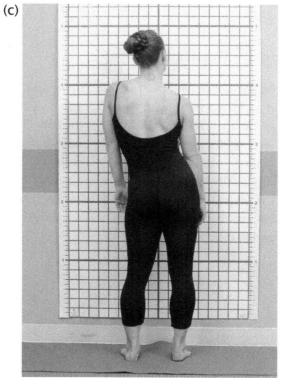

FIGURE 5.2 Continued

scoliosis or idiopathic kyphosis. These conditions require medical guidance and at times might require surgery; however, these conditions can be mitigated with exercises, braces, and mindfulness to daily habits. Most of the time these curves develop as a result of postural habits and overuse. This condition is called postural scoliosis or postural kyphosis. These conditions can be changed through attention to daily movement habits and reconditioning the muscles of the trunk to support a balance in the spinal curves.

The spine can move in four basic ways: flexion, extension, lateral bending, and lateral rotation. Dance forms combine these movements in a myriad of creative ways to elicit nonverbal expression. Developing a nonjudgmental awareness of where your spine moves easily and where it resists movement can open up the possibility to change this pattern to allow for greater ease and potential for movement.

Mindfulness in Dance Class

Just before class starts, practice roll down from the wall, side bending at the wall, and the rotation sequence from the movement exploration above to discover the flexibility of the spine. Or after class let your spine discover neutral from the rigors of class by rolling down from the wall.

Between exercises in class, consider the tripod of the feet and balance of the head, aligning the curves of the spine, and recovering from the joys and demands of twists, turns, side bending, and contractions required in class. It is a moment to pause and press reset for your body.

Mindfulness in Daily Life

Getting out of a car or spiraling out of a chair each day after a meal is a delightful place to engage in the elegant use of the spiral musculature for ease in action. Let your eyes and head lead the turn and let the whole spine follow. Let the body freely move around the spine and press the feet into the floor to help propel you out of the chair.

It is not about getting it right, it is about the opportunity to bring your attention to spiral movements during daily tasks, making the mundane playful and fun. This movement can improve your expressivity in dance class, particularly for work with cambre, upper, middle, and low back curves, contractions, and X roll variations, as well as all the other spiral movements in the body.

6

The Pelvis as Conduit from Head to Feet

One of the most common concerns for dancers is alignment of the pelvis. Dance students frequently complain of hip pain, low back pain, and knee pain. This is often related to mal-coordinated, unconscious movement patterns of the hips in relation to the head, spine, and legs. Inaccurate understanding of pelvic engagement can impede dynamic alignment and inhibit lateral rotation, or turnout. Learning skeletal and muscular landmarks and their relationship to movement patterning can often create a shift in habitual use of the pelvis for more efficient action. Visualizing the anatomical landmarks accurately allows dancers to acknowledge habit and reassess their movement to better support the pelvic structure through the rigors of dance training.

The Story: Ballet Dancer Duck Walk

A talented dancer and dance educator who performed with American Ballet Theater and on the Broadway stage, started to experience chronic pain in her hips while walking and limitations in turnout during passé, retiré, and développé. We noticed two interesting habits in her that were having a significant impact on daily activity and dancing. During her everyday actions and in dance class, her toes were always pointing out to the sides as if she was standing rotated in first or second position. Standing turned out was the norm for her hips and legs, not just the practice during class. Ballet is a beautiful art form that requires rigorous hours of practice, but continuing to turn out all day, every day, actually impedes the resilient balance of the myofascial and neuromuscular system surrounding the hip from performing efficiently, limits range of motion, and can cause pain.

Exploration: Common Mismapping of the Hip Socket

1. Point to where you think your femur, or thigh bone, meets the pelvis at the hip socket.
2. Make a note of this spot. When asked to point to the hip socket, many people are uncertain where this joint is located. They will point to their greater trochanter, located on the thigh or femur bone, or often people point at their waist at the top of the iliac crest.
3. Place your hand on what is commonly known as the hip bone or the iliac crest at the anterior superior iliac spine (ASIS) and begin to move your hand toward the pubic bone. You will feel a softer space or indent. This area is the anterior portion of the ball-and-socket joint of the hip, where the head of the femur rests in the socket called the acetabulum (see Figure 6.1).
4. Leave your fingers here and march in place. You will notice this area folding. This motion is the head of the femur gliding in the socket to allow for hip flexion, and the muscles that primarily flex the hip are located on this anterior side. For many the location of the hip socket is a surprising revelation.

Your Findings and Why They Matter

When one unconsciously has a faulty body map of where a joint action occurs, the brain recruits muscle action based on this inaccurate information and the body then moves

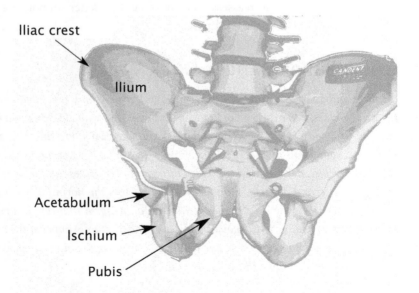

FIGURE 6.1 Skeletal landmarks of the hip. (*Source/author*: https://commons.wikimedia.org/wiki/File:Pelvis_diagram.png [public domain])

inefficiently. Often the lateral or outside muscles of the leg and hip are more developed than the more medial muscles. This unconscious mismapping of the hip in relation to the leg can create a muscular and myofascial imbalance and contribute to snapping hip syndrome, low back pain, a tight iliotibial band, or patella tendinitis (jumper's knee). Fortunately, the brain and body are very adaptable. It is easy to rethink and discover a body map with greater structural integrity. Functional awareness of hip rotation and pelvic alignment are key to improving dance technique and maintaining whole body health over time.

The Anatomy: Skeletal and Muscular Considerations for Pelvic Alignment

The hip joint, or acetabular femoral joint, is a complex structure. It is the conduit from the torso to the legs. It is a ball-and-socket joint. The rounded head of the femur bone fits into the concave structure of the acetabulum of the pelvis. A ball-and-socket joint facilitates flexion, extension, adduction, abduction, medial rotation, and lateral rotation.

Figure 6.1 shows that the acetabulum (hip socket) is midway between the highest ridge of the pelvic bone (ASIS) and the pubis. This location is where you were feeling the indent when you were marching in place during the movement exploration above.

The hip joint has a complex muscular support system. A few key muscles are useful to know for improving dance training and daily balance. One key support muscle for hip flexion that links the torso to the legs is the psoas major, as seen in Figure 6.2. It is the muscle closest to the spine in the front or anterior side and attaches to the bodies of the vertebrae of the spine. The psoas is the deepest muscle anteriorly and is similar to the transversospinalis muscle because it contains stabilizing Type 1 muscle fibers to support the body in upright posture. This muscle interdigitates with the iliacus to form a common tendon called the iliopsoas tendon. The psoas major also contains Type 2 or mobilizing fibers to support movements of dynamic action. It is a strong flexor of the hip and the only muscle that flexes the hip beyond 90 degrees. It is a primary muscle of effective développé as is discussed later in the chapter.

The pelvis has a wide range of movement. It can move through all the positions for jazz isolations. It can sustain an undercurve for a modern dance contraction. The beautiful art form of dance explores the end ranges of movement for the pelvis depending on the aesthetic. The important concept to understand through Functional Awareness® is that the body will be in pain if you maintain these end ranges for too long or carry them into your daily life habits.

Pelvic neutral is not a position. Rather it is a range in which the body can sustain upright balance and sitting with the least amount of stress (Figure 6.3c). Anterior tilt is when the pelvis tips and often exhibits a sway in the low back (lordosis) (Figure 6.3a). Posterior tilt is when the pelvis is tucked under as in a contraction in the low back and looks more like a letter C (Figure 6.3b). Try each pelvic position for yourself and exaggerate the sensation. You will begin to feel where the stress is revealed.

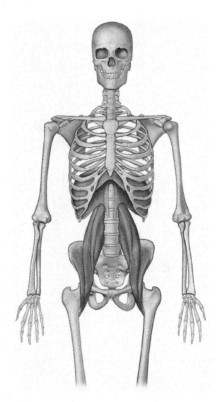

FIGURE 6.2 The psoas and diaphragm. (*Source/author*: Functional Awareness® and artist Caitlin Duck-wall)

Figure 6.3D displays a dancer in forward sway. This position is when the pelvis may be in neutral or tucked under (posterior tilt) and, in addition, the center of gravity has been moved forward toward the balls of the feet too far, upsetting the plumb line of balance in the whole system. In dance this is a common way for dancers to move over the balls of the feet for relevé. Unfortunately, this stance places stress on the low back, knees, and hips. Moving the whole body structure toward equal weight at the tripod of the feet is a more efficient model for dynamic alignment than pushing the pelvis forward. Figure 6.3D demonstrates forward sway while in neutral pelvis. The ABT dancer in the story at the beginning of this chapter was holding on to forward sway all day. This placed undue strain on her hip joint and caused unnecessary wear and discomfort over time.

Try the following movement exploration to discover more about your personal habits in pelvic balance.

Exploration: Anterior Tip, Posterior Tip, and Forward Sway

Begin by practicing some of the anatomical imagery presented in the previous chapters. Consider the tripod of balance at the feet. Allow yourself to imagine the balance of the

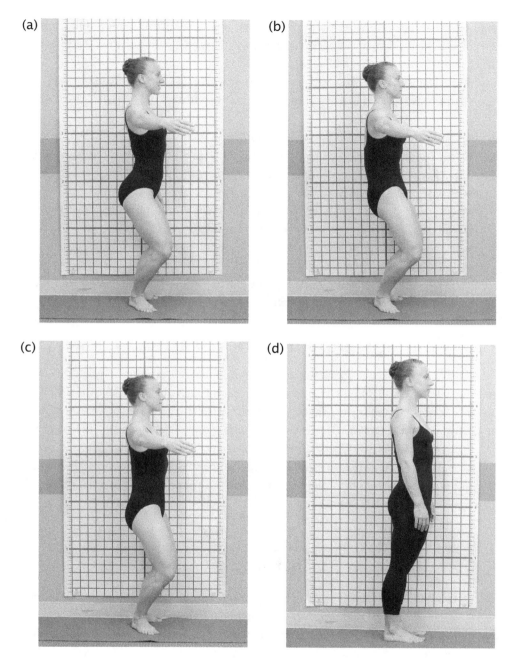

FIGURE 6.3 The pelvis: (A) anterior tilt, (B) posterior tilt, (C) neutral pelvis, (D) forward sway. (*Source/author*: With permission from Jim Burger Photography)

head on the spine and the AO joint. Remember, if you balance at the feet and consider the poise of the head, many unnecessary muscle actions release in order for you to recruit into dynamic alignment with efficiency.

This exercise can be explored on your own or with a partner. If you are working with a partner, ask permission to place your hands on the partner.

1. Partner A stands in parallel position of the feet.
2. Partner B's hands are placed onto the skeletal structures of the pelvis: one hand on the ASIS and one hand gently on the sacrum. The sacrum is the triangular-shaped bone at the base of the spinal vertebrae.
3. Have Partner A bend the knees and straighten them in a plié motion. Partner B, notice if the pelvis tips forward or back in your hands.
4. Partner A goes up on his or her toes in a relevé motion and Partner B senses and observes the change in pelvic position, if any.
5. Partner A considers a neutral place for the pelvis. Partner B, observe if Partner A can maintain that while going through plié and relevé again.

Your Findings and Why They Matter

Pelvic neutral is a place to maintain or move through, not a position to grip. The pelvis and spine do have a slight movement when moving through plié and relevé. If you grip or preserve the position of the pelvis with too much tension, it can place unnecessary strain on the ligaments and tendons, resulting in pain at the front of the hips or in the lower back.

The pelvis is not an isolated structure. Consider the tripod of balance at your feet and the poise of the head before shifting pelvic alignment. Releasing the initial habit, then recruiting necessary muscular support to sustain a dynamic pelvic alignment, creates greater efficiency and less stress.

The Anatomy: Muscular Considerations for Turnout

Lateral rotation (turnout) is a specific aesthetic and requirement in many contemporary and classical dance forms. This movement initiates at the hip socket. The biggest muscular misconception for dancers is that practicing turnout all day improves their turnout. They often consciously or unconsciously walk in turnout, stand in turnout, and sleep turned out. This constant activation of one set of muscle fibers without opportunity for recoil and recuperation places increased stress on the ligaments supporting the hip. In short, standing and walking turned out all the time does not improve turnout. It impedes elasticity and resiliency of joint motion. This is the secondary factor in the ABT dancer's hip restrictions and pain. One of the primary groups of muscles used to recruit turnout

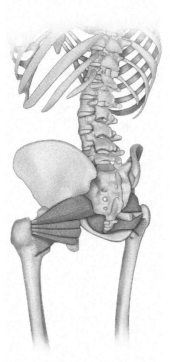

FIGURE 6.4 Deep lateral rotators of the hip. (*Source/author*: Functional Awareness® and artist Caitlin Duckwall)

in the hip are called the deep lateral rotators. The six deep lateral rotators of the hip are the quadratus femoris, obturator externus, obturator internus, superior gemellus, inferior gemellus, and piriformis (see Figure 6.4).

Exploration: Recruiting the Deep Lateral Rotators

1. Repeat previous exploration above, but change the foot position to first or second position turned out.
2. If you have a Balanced Body Rotator Disc, repeat both explorations for neutral pelvis in parallel, first, and second on the discs. The Rotator Disc is very effective for discovering the necessary muscular recruitment needed to sustain turnout.
3. If you do not have a Rotator Disc, wearing a pair of nylon socks can also supply the glide needed to practice the activity in Step 2. Cotton socks are less effective for this exploration. Cotton often has more friction with the floor and not enough slide to permit the femur to rotate in the acetabulum easily.

Exploration: Myofascial Release of Deep Lateral Rotators

1. Find a small ball that you can use for self-massage. The ball can range in hardness from a lacrosse or tennis ball, to a softer ball such as a Nerf ball. Take some time to discover the ideal ball and pressure that works for you.
2. Lie down in semi-supine position, on your back with both knees bent.
3. Place one ball under the right buttocks. Allow for several gentle cycles of breathing in your own timing. Allow the muscle tissue to release around the ball. Let go of tension in this experience.
4. Slide the right leg out gently to straighten the knee with the ball still in place. Pause, allow for a breath, and then return. Do this twice.
5. Let both knees drop to the right while the ball is still in place and take a moment to breathe here in this position.
6. Return to semi-supine and remove the ball. Slide the right leg out to straighten the knee and then the left. Notice if there is a difference between the two legs.
7. Repeat on the other side.

Your Findings and Why They Matter

After performing the exercise on the right leg, did you notice a difference between the right and the left leg? Many people feel the right leg is longer or more relaxed than the left. The sensation often equalizes after performing the exercise on both legs. This exploration releases neuromuscular myofascial tissue to release unnecessary tension and provide resilience in action.

Mindfulness in Dance Class

As you practice a dance phrase during class, be consciously aware of the various movements needed in the pelvis. Experiment with pelvic neutral during a phrase that travels across the floor. Investigate the various other pelvic tilts that are possible (anterior tilt, posterior tilt, forward sway). Different dance forms employ many possible pelvic orientations depending on that style of movement. Observe the choreographer's intention and bring a clarity regarding the pelvis to your dancing. At the end of the exploration in the dance phrase, return to pelvic neutral as well as an awareness of the tripod of the feet and the balance of the head to allow for recuperation and restoration.

Mindfulness in Daily Life

If you practice dynamic alignment in dance class but ignore it the rest of the day, it compromises the progress your body can make toward improving range of motion and technical skills in dance training. While brushing your teeth or doing dishes, notice your feet and gently move them toward neutral.

In addition notice your habitual stance for pelvic tilt. Without judgment, assess this pelvic tilt and gently shift your body toward a balanced neutral. As a tool for discovering neutral pelvis, return to your tripod of the feet and balance at the AO joint. Notice if your pelvis finds its way back to neutral without having to create the position. If it needs more encouragement, picture the bony landmarks of your pelvis and allow for ease in action. Asking yourself to make this pelvic shift in daily use will deepen your motor sensory map for pelvic neutral, and improve your ability to access this pelvic support during dance practice and performance.

Ways of Walking
How Gait Affects Dance Training

Walking is propelling the body's center of gravity, or plumb line of standing, forward in space. Walking is an effective recuperation tool and whole health activity. We learn to walk when we are very young, yet we are never taught how to do so biomechanically. Movement patterns that form, as early as crawling, affect our skeletal structure, muscle structure, and myofascial tissue. Walking, like standing, can promote balance, or it can systemically compromise the spine and become a source of discomfort. Habit plays an important role in the choices one makes for walking. Functional Awareness® works with people to retrain walking patterns to enable greater efficiency and stability.

The Story: Allegra and the Cobbler

I live in Brooklyn, New York. In the city it is common for people to take more than 10,000 steps per day! With that much walking, anyone would need to send his or her shoes to a cobbler. This is why there are shoe repair places all over New York City. I have a pair of boots that I love. I continually need the soles replaced, so I can continue to wear them even after I've worn out the soles. On my third trip to replace the heels of my boots, Victor, the cobbler, pointed out that I am constantly wearing out one spot on my left heel more than the rest. Aha! This was an amazing observation, since I regularly have left ankle pain and discomfort. My shoes were a clue to what my habit was in walking and the reason for my discomfort in my ankle. I strike heavily on the outside of my left heel more than my right and not evenly through my foot. Thanks to Victor, I had a better understanding of what my habit was in walking.

The act of walking is a combination of our structure, our understanding of function, and our habitual body actions. One delight in being human is our systems are very adaptable to change. Knowing a bit about how "the suit fits," allows us to reconsider how walking affects dancing. Take a look at the bottom of your favorite shoes. Where are they worn out? Does this reflect where you keep your weight in walking and standing?

The first thing we look at when working with injured dancers is walking. As discussed in Chapter 6, using the turnout muscles or deep lateral rotators of the hip constantly in everyday life impedes natural hip function, places undo stress on the lower back and sacroiliac joint, and creates wear at the iliofemoral ligament. Walking with the toes pointed out is a common habit for many people. This constant recruitment of the deep lateral rotators can create less resilience in the hip structure. It does not improve dance skills. It just feels comfortable, as it is how your "suit fits." In repatterning walking you can regain bilateral range of rotation as well as improve stability on the standing leg.

Exploration: Stepping into Someone Else's Shoes

This activity can be done in partners or without a partner by recording yourself and watching the video.

1. Partner A begins by standing in a comfortable stance. Partner B first observes this body stance from a side view and then from the back or posterior view.
2. Partner A begins to walk around the room and Partner B follows, imitating or mirroring the walk of the person in front.
3. Partner A begins to notice asymmetry or idiosyncrasies about his or her own walk. Partner A starts to exaggerate these so they become evident to Partner B, who is following behind. Partner B takes on these new exaggerations.
4. Partner A increases the exaggeration a little more with Partner B following behind.
5. Finally Partner A steps away while Partner B continues to walk, in order for Partner A to see his or her exaggerated habit. Discuss your findings.

Your Findings and Why They Matter

As noted in standing, small unconscious habits create subtle imbalances in walking as well. We do not feel them as pain often during the day, but the repercussions from these habits affect the system. If you walk for 5 minutes in an exaggerated manner of your habit, you reveal the muscle stress that would occur in regular walking over the course of a day. This movement exploration demonstrates the muscular impact your habits have on the body.

The Anatomy: An Introduction to Biomechanical Considerations in Gait

Gait, or walking, is as complex as a leap or turn in dancing. Each person has a unique walk, and in coaching gait efficiency, there is not one set of tips to address everyone's issues. It is useful to become functionally aware of a few key points within gait to elicit greater ease and balance. This mindfulness will aid the body in recuperation from activity instead of contributing imbalanced action to fatigue the body further.

Walking involves movement through the whole body. We will take a closer look specifically at the motions required of the hip, knee, and ankle. The ankle (talocrural joint), a synovial hinge joint, has the potential for flexion and extension. Other movements such as rolling out (inversion) or rolling in (eversion), are actually movements that occur in the other thirty joints of the foot. The knee, as a hinge joint, mostly moves through flexion and extension (though it does have about 3 to 5 degrees of rotation on average available for resiliency). The hip, as a ball-and-socket joint, has a large range of motion and has the potential for many different actions: flexion, extension, abduction, adduction, and medial and lateral rotation. Walking is a movement predominantly forward in the sagittal plane; thus all three joints in the leg have to move through flexion and extension to create the gait cycle.

The gait cycle begins when one foot strikes the ground in front of you and it ends when the same foot strikes the ground again. There are two phases in gait: the stance phase and the swing phase (Figure 7.1).

Stance Phase

Stance phase occurs when a foot is in contact with the earth. This phase includes the initial heel strike of the foot in dorsiflexion on the ground, a rolling through the weight of the foot, and then propulsion off the ball of the foot in plantarflexion to propel the leg to begin to swing forward.

Swing Phase

Swing phase is when the foot is not in contact with the earth and the leg is literally swinging from extension to flexion. Once the foot propels off in the back, the leg swings freely to travel forward.

This seemingly simple motion truly involves the whole body from heels to head. Flexion and extension occur at the ankle, the knee, and the hip. Rotation occurs as a

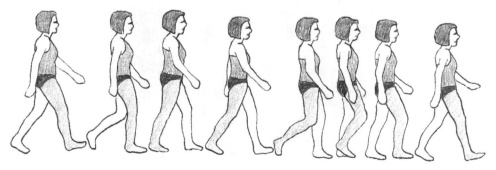

FIGURE 7.1 Phases of the gait cycle. (*Source/artist*: Hollis McCracken)

ripple effect up the spine and flexion and extension reverberate into the shoulder joint to create the swinging of our arms. There are many places throughout our bodies in which we can slightly alter our gait to create grinding, pulling, twisting, straining, or misalignment in the body. The moment the leg moves into slight medial or lateral rotation and does not track correctly, strain is put on the entire leg structure and can create pain over time. Recall the habits you noted in standing; how would these very same habits affect your walking? As we mature, we develop idiosyncrasies in our walking habits. As seen in the cobbler story, these idiosyncrasies are sometimes evident by looking at the bottom of the shoes you wear most frequently while walking. You discovered some of these in the walking exploration. These habits can facilitate ease of motion or they can compromise the system. The following exploration is one approach to discovering easeful walking through Functional Awareness®, to allow for a release from habit, and an opportunity to choose new patterns stepping forward.

Exploration: Biomechanical Ease in Walking

1. Start to walk. Notice what part of your body leads out first. Many of us lead with our face or push forward with the pelvis. Some people flick a straight leg out first. What do you notice? Keep this in mind to notice if this is happening today or if it is a frequent habit.

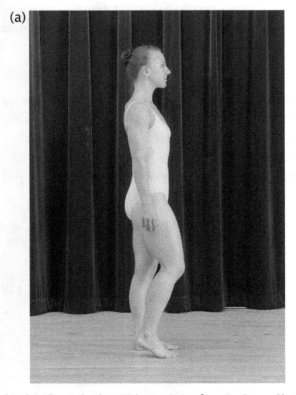

(a)

FIGURE 7.2 Peel and pedal. (*Source/author*: With permission from Jim Burger Photography)

(b)

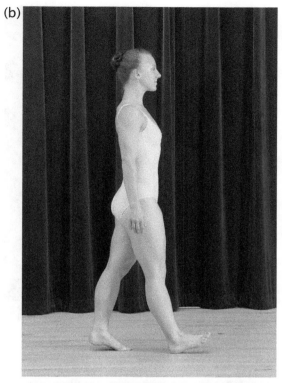

(c)

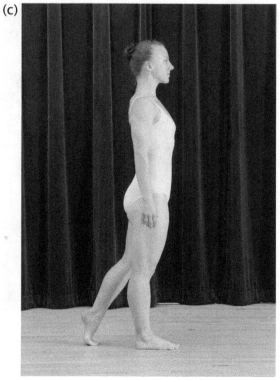

FIGURE 7.2 Continued

(d)

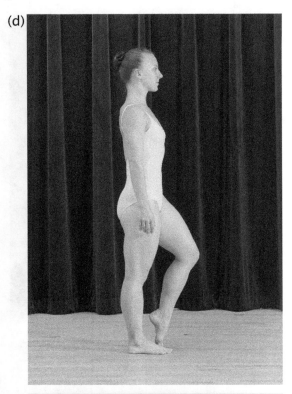

(e)

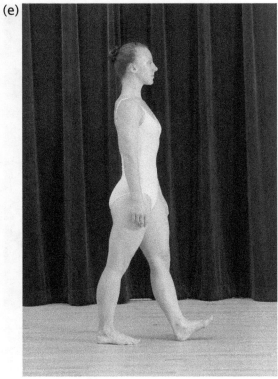

FIGURE 7.2 Continued

2. Stand once again with equal weight on both legs. Consider the tripod of balance at the feet and gaze out at eye level to visualize the AO joint and poise of the head. Think up, not down.

3. Recruit for efficient motor control. Slightly shift your weight to the right leg as you peel your left foot off the floor and propel or push off the ball of the left foot (see Figure 7.2). This is called *peel and pedal*. Continue to peel and pedal from one leg to the other.

4. When walking, the knee should be the first body part to break the plane forward, not the face and head or the pelvis.

5. The most common issue for people who experience pain from walking and running is their over stride, taking steps that swing too far from the body's center of gravity. Try smaller steps at a quicker tempo when you are in a hurry instead of large steps that overexert the system.

Mindfulness in Dance Class

Large strides with turned-out legs during leaps and runs are beautiful and part of the aesthetics in some forms of dance. Recover from that required action in everyday life by letting the feet be more toward parallel and the stride to balance within an easeful leg swing.

During a traveling phrase across the floor, notice what part of the body leads. Does your habit for initiating the movement lead first? Can you pause, allow for a breath, and rethink the movement initiation required for that phase?

Mindfulness in Daily Life

As you walk from your car into work or into the dance class, take a moment to "think up" instead of down to lengthen the back of your body from heel to head. Next allow the many joints of the lower limb to bring you to your destination as you peel and pedal. Notice the rhythm of your foot strike. Is the rhythm even from left to right or do you favor one side more than the other? Think about this rhythm in your body and see if it allows the body to become more symmetrical pedal-a-pedal-a-pedal-a-pedal-a.

Check your own shoes to see if they wear out more on one shoe more than the other. Does it wear more on one portion of the foot? How does this observation relate to the movement explorations performed earlier? What can you discover about how you move through life?

Breath as the Deep Central Support for Dancing

One of the fundamental systems of the body is the respiratory system. We breathe automatically and unconsciously. We also can use the breathing mechanism in intricate ways with conscious control. For example, singers, horn players, and actors control breath to achieve amazing artistic results. The breathing mechanism supports neuromuscular stamina and cardiovascular health. Breathing is not always a fundamental aspect of many forms of dance training, yet it is at the heart of creating expressivity and phrasing in all forms of dance.

Breath is both autonomic and muscularly controlled. As we have musculoskeletal habits, we also have unconscious habits for breathing. Exploring a few functional principles for respiratory action in relation to breathing habit provides possibilities to improve respiratory function, reduce excess tension and stress, and improve expressivity in movement.

The Story: Breath Support in Performance

We were attending a choral concert of young talented middle school singers from the entire county in Maryland. The auditorium was packed with parents and friends of these aspiring vocal artists on a warm Sunday in May. As they began the second piece on the program, one of the singers suddenly fainted, but safely came to sit on the bleachers. The singer was helped by a parent, and the conductor moved along through the piece. We could see the anxiety in the students rise along with their adrenaline from being onstage, and they began to then tighten in their backs and knees and tense in their vocal system. As the program progressed, another student fainted, and then another, and another. It resembled the hysteria of the Salem witch trials with young women dropping left and right until there were parents onstage along the sides of the bleachers to help students who fainted to recover safely. All the while the choral director was attempting to let the show go on. At intermission the *students were in a panic about returning to the stage again for fear they might faint. Under the anxiety and stress, students began to tighten the low back and knees. This action inhibits the diaphragmatic movement needed for singing. In turn the students were taking air in predominantly through the mouth, leading to CO_2 accumulation in the lungs and a condition often referred to as shallow water blackout, which caused them to faint. A little functional awareness could have avoided this situation easily as you will discover in this chapter.*

Exploration: Discovering Your Preferences for Breathing

This exploration in experiential anatomy can be performed in a chair or semi-supine on a mat (lying down on the floor with knees bent). It is useful to have a notebook nearby to record your observations as suggested periodically throughout the movement exploration.

Part 1

Take a moment to locate your lungs on the skeleton chart provided (Figure 8.1) or just visualize where your lungs are in your torso. Write down a bit about what you know about the lungs, the diaphragm, and breathing. It may be that you have some prior understand-

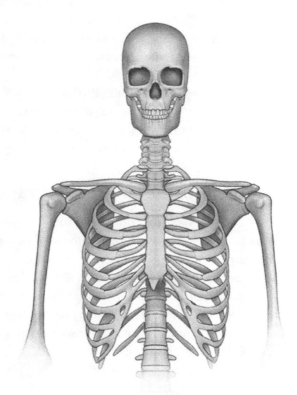

FIGURE 8.1 Rib cage. (*Source/author*: Functional Awareness® and artist Caitlin Duckwall)

ing about the breathing mechanism or you may only know that smoking is bad for the lungs. There is no judgment in what you know. It is a starting point of reference for your explorations, a baseline for your current knowledge.

Part 2

This guided movement exploration is a Romita-designed practice to improve awareness of breathing patterns. For an audio guide of this activity, see www.functionalawareness. org/.

1. Notice your breathing. Visualize where you see your breath going as it comes into the body and its journey through to exhale.
2. Notice the length of your inhalations and exhalations. You might use a counting system to give yourself a relative measure of time for both.
3. Inhale through the nose and exhale out the mouth; inhale through the mouth and exhale out the nose; inhale and exhale through the nose; or inhale and exhale through the mouth. Note how you prefer to breathe.
4. Where is the tip of your tongue resting? Where is the belly of the tongue resting? Stop and sit up and record what you have noticed thus far.

The Anatomy: Skeletal and Muscular Considerations for Breathing

Many people have a cortical map or body map with the lungs lower in the rib cage and smaller. The unconscious mismap of the lungs and misperceptions about breathing provide idiosyncratic breathing patterns and a lack of general efficiency in breathing. This inefficient breathing pattern has an effect on musicality and expressivity in dance.

The lungs begin at the first rib, just above the collarbone or clavicle, and inferiorly rest between the fourth and fifth rib (Figure 8.2). So "breathing into your belly" is not an anatomical function. It is a lovely metaphor to encourage muscular support for breathing, but it also can lead to misunderstanding. There is muscular support for breath in the lower portion of the torso, but there are no lungs in this region. In the front, or anteriorly, the ribs have greater expansion because of the costal cartilage. The true ribs (1 to 7) have the least mobility because they attach directly to the sternum. The false ribs (8 through 10) and the floating ribs (11 and 12) have greater mobility. The diaphragm drapes from the top of the dome at the fourth rib and attaches along the false ribs.

The diaphragm interdigitates with the psoas major. The psoas major is one of the muscles from Chapter 3 that provides postural support and hip flexion. The psoas originates at the twelfth thoracic vertebra where its fibers weave with those of the diaphragm. The psoas major continues along the front of the spine and attaches onto a knob on the inside of the upper thigh known as the lesser trochanter. In other words, how you stand and maintain the pelvic tilt has a profound effect on breathing. For a moment stand up

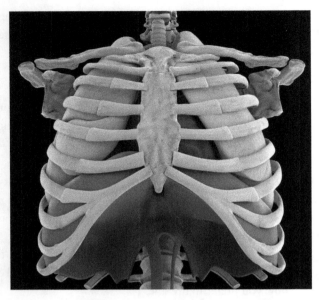

FIGURE 8.2 Location of lungs in thoracic cage. (*Source/author*: Shutterstock)

with an anterior tilt or sway back and lock your knees. Try to take a deep breath in. Now release the knees and return to a neutral pelvis and try another inhale. You might notice quite a difference in the ability to take in the air. This inability to take in air was what was happening to the middle school choral students. With knees and back tight, the psoas would not allow the diaphragm to easefully expand and contract. See the connection between these two muscles in Figure 6.2.

Exploration: Breathing Patterns
Part 1
Become acquainted with the specific breathing approach in this activity. Inhale through the nose and then exhale out the mouth, making an "sssss" or "sh" sound. Practice this several times. It will be used through the entirety of this exploration.

1. Place your hands at your lower abdomen and pelvis and allow yourself to observe the movement in the lower part of your torso using the "sss" or "sh" breathing. Do not force anything to happen. Notice if there is movement under your hands or in the lower abdomen.
2. Place your hands on your upper ribs. Do this by crossing your arms across your chest so each hand lands on the opposite side of the rib cage. Inhale through the nose, with the "sss" or "sh" sound to exhale. Notice if there is movement in this region of the body underneath your fingers. Sense the movement of the intercostal muscles

moving into three-dimensional expansion on the inhalation and releasing from expansion on the exhalation.

3. Place your hands on your collarbone and upper chest and breathe into the upper lungs or auxiliary respiratory system. Notice the movement in the cervical spine as you inhale and exhale.

4. Finally place your thumbs under your armpits and visualize breath traveling to the lungs, which are by the upper ribs. Place your hands gently around your neck and see if there is movement in the neck as you breathe. Record your discoveries.

Part 2

1. Allow for breath while thinking of the spine as a stainless steel rod from between your ears down to your tailbone. Sense how this feels.

2. Now change the image to the spine as a soft weeping willow branch and the breath is like the wind.

3. Think of the spine as seaweed and notice how this shifts your breath.

4. Finally move to child pose and let yourself breathe into the posterior portion of your lungs.

5. Record your findings.

Your Findings and Why They Matter

Discovering your habitual function for breathing allows for an increased awareness of your patterns of use. Learning some key components about the anatomical function allows you to make different choices to explore greater freedom in movement.

If you sense movement when your hands are on the ribs, your breathing preference is using more intercostal activity and less the diaphragm and psoas for action. Some people prefer to gasp air in through the mouth. This action can overuse the muscles of the neck. The spine is not a stainless steel rod, but rather a series of vertebrae and discs that allow for movement, more like a spring than a rod. On inhalation or inspiration the spine moves into a slight arching of the neck, chest, and low back. On exhalation the muscles return to the stasis of the spine. The rotatores and multifidus muscles of the transverso-spinalis encourage a small bit of movement between each vertebra.

Mindfulness in Dance Class

Lift the head and chest into extension (a back cambré in ballet or a suspension in contemporary dance). Notice your breath in response to this action. Many students hold their breath when arching their back, which can sometimes cause a brief dizziness or seeing stars. An inhalation can support this motion. To return the spine to upright, release the head with a slight nod of the chin as you exhale to return. Is this different than your habit?

How does awareness of your breathing patterns affect the musicality of breath? Explore this in class by performing a phrase without thinking of your breath, and then later return it with breath purposely choreographed into the phrase.

Mindfulness in Daily Life

Before you sleep, practice the three cycles of breathing to allow for a mindful enlivening of the breathing system before rest. Notice your preference for breathing when you are tired, happy, sad, or excited. Observe the changes in how you are holding your body in relation to breath. If you change your breathing, does this change your body or your mood at all?

Master dance educator and Certified Movement Analyst Peggy Hackney speaks eloquently about the breathing mechanism in her book *Making Connections* (see Further Readings):

> We breathe automatically, but breath can be influenced by and is reflective of changes in consciousness, feelings, and thoughts . . . The key element in usefulness of medical-scientific information to increase movement facility is the degree to which it facilitates a more lively moving image of physiological or neuromuscular connections within the body (pp. 51–60).

Core Support

Core support is the skeletal, muscular, and myofascial recruitment needed to maintain a balanced center of gravity (COG) in any position. Core support involves coordinated alignment and multiple muscle actions. The muscles of the "core" are not solely the superficial muscles of our abdomen, such as the "'six pack'" rectus abdominis and the obliques; the core muscles are all around the trunk—front, back, and side—and include muscles that are very deep, close to the spine. These deep muscles of the trunk include the psoas and transversospinalis group, mentioned in Chapter 3, as well as the muscles of the pelvic floor. When the balance between the feet and the head is not coordinated, the fast twitch (Type 2) mobilizing muscle fibers of the transversus abdominis, internal and external obliques, and rectus abdominis will have ineffective value in movement function. However, when the fast twitch mobilizing muscle works in concert with the transversospinalis, the diaphragm, and the action in the pelvic floor, it facilitates a dynamic synergy for efficient use of the body in action. The central musculoskeletal support system that stabilizes the trunk and also mobilizes the torso for action is referred to as central support in Functional Awareness®.

The Story: Sometimes Less Is More

A dance major was in chronic low back pain and her diagnosis was muscle strain in the low back. She attended sessions in physical therapy that aided in her recovery. Although this therapy relieved the pain for a while, the chronic back pain still recurred. In assessing her standing, a gentle hand was placed on her low back and pelvis. The dancer was holding her abdominal muscles very tightly, so tightly it was pushing her pelvis into posterior tilt. This stance, in turn, hyperextended the upper back and the weight of the thoracic spine was congregating at the low back where she reported pain. In some ways she was trying too hard to fix muscle weaknesses by gripping or overusing the superficial core musculature. A resilient body for dancing develops a balance between recruitment and release, between exertion and recuperation. Understanding abdominal support in relation to the pelvic floor and the plumb line of balance from head to feet enabled the dance major to move into a more resilient dynamic alignment and relieved her chronic pain. Efficiency in action sometimes requires the dancer to do less to achieve more.

Exploration: What Is Core or Central Support?

Consider your baseline of knowledge for core support:

1. What is your current understanding of the muscles of core support?
2. What exercises, if any, do you practice frequently to address core support?

There are many excellent programs for conditioning the body to strengthen core support. Functional Awareness˚ is not about conditioning. FA develops greater sensory and cognitive understanding for the central support in order for the conditioning practices to be more effective, and FA provides simple, mindful practices in daily tasks to help sustain the benefits from those rigorous core workouts of your choice.

In Functional Awareness˚ the investigation of anatomical function for the central or core support begins deep in the torso and then progresses to the more superficial muscular structures. The core is a series of muscular layers that work in concert to sustain the body in upright posture, aid in all motions of the trunk, and function to enable efficient lifting, swinging, and partnering. They sustain the integrity of the body in action. The deepest muscles for central support are examined in detail in Chapter 3, the transversospinalis. In carrying over the lessons from the previous chapters, it is important to consider the plumb line of balance to engage core spinal support from the rotatores, multifidus, and semispinalis group on the posterior trunk while the psoas provides deep postural support on the anterior portion of the trunk. Another group of deep support muscles, at the base of the pelvis, are the muscles of the pelvic floor.

The Anatomy: Pelvic Floor

The pelvic floor refers to the muscular structure that spans across the inferior portion of the pelvis from the pubic bone to the coccyx, from ilium to coccyx, and connects the pelvis to the legs from the sacrum to the greater trochanter on the femur, and from the ischial bones to the greater trochanter.

These muscles, seen in the Figure 9.1, form a supportive hammock for the skeletal pelvic bowl. It is important to maintain an elasticity and resiliency in the pelvic floor muscles for several reasons. These muscles control urinary function, so they therefore maintain urinary track health. The pelvic floor muscles enhance sexual satisfaction as the muscles in orgasm. The pelvic floor also provides a hammock of muscular support for the internal organs in the lower abdomen.

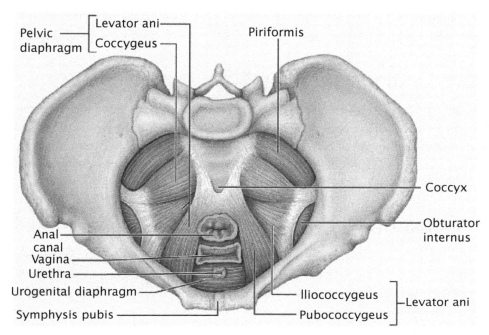

FIGURE 9.1 Muscles of the pelvic floor. (*Source/author*: Shutterstock)

The levator ani, coccygeus, piriformis, and obturator muscles of the pelvic floor are important for dancers because they coordinate with breath to support action to move the pelvis during standing in parallel or turned out, traveling forward in space, and changing directions. The muscles of the pelvic floor are an internal steering mechanism for propelling the body.

Exploration: Sensing the Muscles of the Pelvic Floor

The muscles of the pelvic floor aid in stabilizing dancers in movement. They also regulate the flow of urine out of the body. To begin to feel these muscles and how they work, try this the next time you use the bathroom to urinate.

1. Begin the flow of urine.
2. Stop and hold the flow for a couple of seconds.
3. Let the flow begin again.
4. Repeat this several times.

You are activating the muscles of the pelvic floor. Discover these muscles while in dance class. Try activating these muscles during the day or in dance class. Explore an easy support from these muscles. Do not over-contract. Recruit the muscles for action, but do not grip. Remember it is the natural recruit and then release of muscle fiber that allow for maximum resiliency for dancing.

Your Findings and Why They Matter

For some this activity allows you to sense the pelvic floor for the first time. This is important for the health reasons described earlier. For others this activity may help refine their understanding of the pelvic floor in a kinesthetic manner, and you can use this muscle function to support the standing leg in balance or aid in propelling the pelvis through space.

The Anatomy: The Psoas Major

The psoas major is another deep muscular component of central support. As discussed previously, the psoas is a deep muscle that supports the stability of the spine and provides resiliency in pelvic movement. As you look at Figure 9.2, you can see that the fibers of the

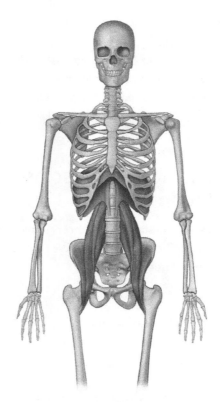

FIGURE 9.2 Psoas major and the diaphragm. (*Source/author*: Functional Awareness® and artist Caitlin Duckwall)

psoas major lie in the sides of the pelvic bowl and merge with the iliacus, connecting the trunk to the legs through the iliopsoas tendon. If this muscle is overly tight and unable to engage in both recruitment and release, your abdominal exercises will demonstrate unsatisfactory results. It is hard to touch this muscle because it rests behind the internal organs of the lower body. One can sense the changes in the body when the psoas releases.

Exploration: Releasing the Psoas Major from Habitual Contraction

1. Stand easily and move through a few développés in parallel. Notice the ease or discomfort as the hip flexes to bring the knee and foot into position.
2. Move to the floor lying on your back in semi-supine. Take a moment to allow the body to rest into the floor, letting the body yield to gravity. Let your jaw release away from your upper teeth.
3. Place a rolled up towel transversely where the sacrum meets the lumbar spine. This maintains your natural lumbar curves while lying down.
4. Take a few minutes to rest here, noticing your breathing and asking yourself to let go of any unnecessary tension. Allow three cycles of breathing in and out using the "sss" or "sh" sound from Chapter 8 to slow down the exhale.
5. Slowly extend your right knee to straighten the leg along the floor. Easily slide the leg back to a semi-supine position. This movement is inspired by the Bartenieff Fundamental Pre-thigh Lift. Repeat this action one more time on the right.
6. Extend your left knee to straighten the leg. Easily slide the leg back to a semi-supine position. Repeat this action again on the left.
7. Gently remove the towel, and let the low back begin to rest into contact with the floor.
8. Roll gently onto one side in a fetal position. Bring awareness to your breathing for several cycles of inspiration and expiration.
9. Slowly move to standing. Try the retiré and développé again and see if there is any difference in sensation. Record your findings mentally or on paper.

Your Findings and Why They Matter

Releasing the habitual tension of the psoas major can heighten a more dynamic connection from the feet through the pelvic floor to the head. This muscle, as seen in previous chapters, has several key roles in movement function. It supports the body in upright posture, it is a primary hip flexor, and it interdigitates with the fibers of the diaphragm to support breathing. Therefore the psoas is a pivotal muscle for central support. This exploration with the towel releases the tension in the psoas major to create more resiliency and ease in action. It is another way to move out of habit, allowing for greater choice in movement.

The Anatomy: Transversus Abdominis

The transversus abdominis encircles the torso from the back near the lumbar spine (at the thoracocolumbar fasciae and costal bones seven to twelve), and wraps around to the front of the body and attaches along the whole front of the torso, from the inferior tip of the breastbone, called the xiphoid process, along the strong tendon sheath of the linea alba to the pubic bone. The transversus abdominis creates a girdle to support the torso from ribs to hips. It also has fibers that interconnect with the diaphragm. If you do not engage the transversus abdominis effectively, your stability in the lower back and pelvis is compromised.

Superficial to the transversus abdominis are the internal and external obliques. These muscles support side bending and spiral movements of the trunk. The diagonal fibers of the internal and external obliques aid in twisting and contribute to central support. Alongside the transversus abdominis in Figure 9.3 is the most superficial abdominal muscle, the rectus abdominis. This muscle originates at the xiphoid process of the sternum and travels along the front of the abdomen to the pubic bone. It is often referred to as the six-pack muscle. Together these muscles are the primary mobilizers of the torso, capable of supporting the body in wonderful actions that require strength and agility.

Exploration: Discovering Your Transversus Abdominis

1. The transversus abdominis is one of the primary muscles you can feel when you cough. Place your hand on your belly and cough a few times. You will feel a muscle

(a)   (b)

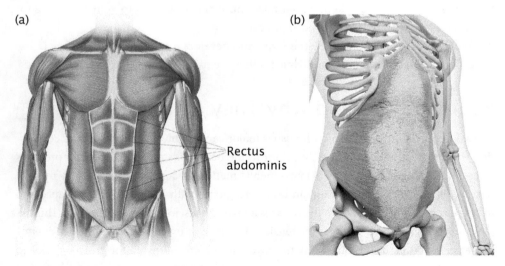

Rectus abdominis

FIGURE 9.3 (a) Rectus abdominis (*Source/author*: Functional Awareness® and artist Caitlin Duckwall) (b) tranversus abdominis. (*Source/author*: Shutterstock)

pulling in. This is the tranversus abdominis aiding the diaphragm to help expel forced air from your lungs. If you hold it too tightly, it inhibits breathing.

2. Perform any abdominal series of your choosing. Exhale on the action that requires the flexion of the trunk. Add an audible "haa" sound for each exhalation to expel the air more forcibly. This sound ensures engagement of the transversus abdominis in action.

Exploration: Discovering Your Rectus Abdominis

The rectus abdominis is the muscle that is engaged when you do a standard "crunch." This is a good exercise to feel the concentric contraction of this muscle. The following exploration investigates the eccentric action of the rectus abdominis.

1. Begin in semi-supine. Reach your arms over your head and sit up in one count.
2. With arms extended forward begin to release your chin to the chest and roll down to the floor in eight slow counts, keeping the knees bent and the feet completely on the floor. Think about each vertebra connecting sequentially to the floor as you lower in these eight slow counts.
3. Make note if you skip some sections of the spine as you roll down. This may indicate where your back is tight or less flexible and your front or anterior trunk is less stable.
4. Repeat Steps 1 through 4 several times.

These abdominal exercises also strengthen the more superficial rectus abdominis to ensure greater stability for the back and torso when lifting, carrying, or supporting your own weight during floor work. Plank and side plank are also excellent exercises to engage the central support system and develop greater stability through the center/core of the body.

Your Findings and Why They Matter

Your breathing is inextricably linked to the central or core neuromuscular and myofascial support systems. Holding the belly in too tightly can restrict breathing and impose restrictions on your ability to have a strong central support system for dancing.

Mindfulness in Dance Class

1. Let the anatomical imagery of the pelvic floor and your experience to engage these muscles buoy you during an exercise or phrase in class. See how this changes your experience with the movement. Does it also change stability or phrasing?

2. If asked to pull up in your belly during a standing exercise in dance class, support the transversus abdominis at 30 percent of its contraction ability. Save the greater contraction of the transversus abdominis muscle for movements that require strength. Constant over-engagement restricts action and expressivity instead of enhancing your skill.

Mindfulness in Daily Life

Think of a supportive hammock of the pelvic floor supporting your pelvis finding balance when you're going about your day—no need to suck in, just think of the pelvis moving up.

10

Expressivity of Arms

The arm structure has complex skeletal features, joint articulations, and many muscular attachments to the trunk. This structure enables a wide variety of expressive movements for the arms. Gesture is an intricate element of artistic expression in dance. Inadvertently a dancer can restrict their possible full range of movement for gesture. Dancers can have a tendency to have their shoulders rolled forward in the glenohumeral joint or shoulder socket. This restricts free and easy range of motion of the arms.

The Story: To Sleep, Perchance to Dream

Jennifer mentioned during dance technique class that she was experiencing restricted movement in her shoulder. She was finding it more and more difficult to raise her arm overhead for any movements in class. Physical therapy, specific exercises, and taping the shoulder proved useful, but the issue was not fully resolving. I asked Jennifer about her daily activities, and then asked her about her sleep position. Jennifer explained that she slept on her side in a fetal position. She did not sleep on the side with her restricted shoulder pressing into the bed. This was helpful because she was not adding additional pressure to the shoulder while sleeping; however, she was hanging her shoulder forward in an unsupported manner and placing strain on the tendons and ligaments (see Figure 10.1).

Often it is not the rigorous activity of dance causing muscular imbalance; it is in dance class that the symptom or restriction becomes more apparent. We sleep for six to nine hours nightly. Certain sleep postures can create imbalances in the neuromuscular and myofascial systems. For Jennifer, sleeping on one side exacerbated the imbalance in the shoulder and arm structure. A supportive pillow to prevent the shoulder from rolling forward during the night reinforced the balance she was working to maintain. This simple prop of the pillow supported her sleep cycle and her arm structure to assist in regaining full range of motion. Functional Awareness® is a series of kinesthetic tools for listening and sensing the body during dance class and outside of dance class . . . even in sleep!

FIGURE 10.1 Sleep position. (*Source/author*: With permission from Jim Burger Photography)

Exploration: Axial Integrity to Support Appendicular Action of the Arms

1. Sit in a slump or C-curve, resting on your sacrum and sense your shoulders curl in response to this.
2. Bring your arms to first position with the fingertips about the height of your belly button.
3. Attempt to bring your arms overhead into fifth position. What do you notice?
4. Now undo the slump, allow for a breath, and move into an easeful yet long spine. Think of a warm sun at the center of the chest and let the sunbeams radiate from that central point all the way out to the fingertips. Repeat the movement of arms from first to fifth position overhead. How does coming to upright balance in sitting affect the ease of movement in the arms?
5. Try this same activity when standing.

Your Findings and Why They Matter

Curling into fetal or sitting in a C-curve is a useful capability and necessary in some forms of dance expression (e.g., contraction). This action involves elevation and forward tilt of the scapula and the ball of the humerus rotates anteriorly forward in the glenohumeral joint. When we leave dance class to go to school, work, or rest at home in front of the computer or TV, we can unwittingly spend hours in this slump, which reinforces a restriction in the expressivity and range of motion of the arms. The ability to shift, change, choose, and adapt is the key to resiliency and discovering your full movement potential.

The Anatomy: Biomechanical Distinctions of the Glenohumeral Joint and Scapula

The arm structure is part of the appendicular skeleton and is comprised of the clavicle, scapula, humerus, radius, and ulna. The arm structure skeletally attaches to the axial skeleton at one point, where the clavicle meets the sternum portion of the rib cage: the sternoclavicular joint. The acromioclavicular joint is at the top of the shoulder where the scapula meets the clavicle (Figure 10.2, A and B). The glenohumeral joint, where the head of the humerus meets the glenoid fossa, is commonly referred to as the shoulder joint.

Muscular Support for Arms

The primary muscles supporting the glenohumeral joint are the four muscles of the rotator cuff, the supraspinatus, infraspinatus, teres minor, and subscapularus (Figure 10.3). Each of these muscles connects the glenohumeral ball-and-socket joint to the rest of the

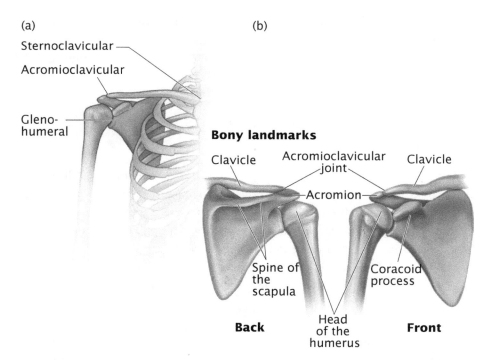

FIGURE 10.2 Skeletal landmarks of the upper arm structure. (*Source/author*: Functional Awareness® and artist Caitlin Duckwall)

Rotator Cuff Muscles

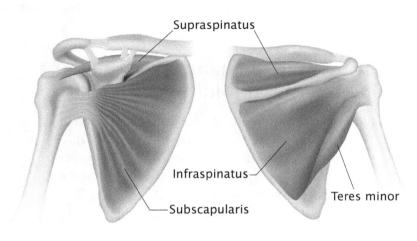

FIGURE 10.3 Muscles of the rotator cuff. (*Source/author*: Shutterstock)

torso and supports its full range of action. The latissimus dorsi, the trapezius muscles on the posterior torso, and the pectoralis major on the front are large superficial muscles that stabilize the trunk (Figure 10.4). The latissimus spans the wide swath of the back and then spirals to insert onto the front of the upper arm at the upper third of the bicipital ridge. The pectoralis major spans across the front of the chest from the sternum and also attaches to the upper third of the bicipital ridge of the humerus.

Exploration: The Eight Motions of the Scapula

1. This exploration can be performed on your own trying Steps a through h, 2 and 3. The activity may also be performed with partners. In pairs, Partner A stands in front of Partner B. Partner B places his or her hands on the scapula of Partner A. This placement will provide a tactile sensory experience of the gliding movement that the scapula performs to support arm and shoulder movement.
   a. Elevation: Lift the shoulder blades up toward your ears.
   b. Depression: Press the shoulder blades back down along the ribs.
   c. Adduction (retraction): Pull the shoulder blades in toward the spine.
   d. Abduction (protraction): Move the shoulder blades away from the spine.
   e. Upward rotation: The natural swing of the inferior tip of the scapula is to swing away from the spine and upward. Bring the fingertips from touching the side seams of the pants and move the arms out in front to first position and then

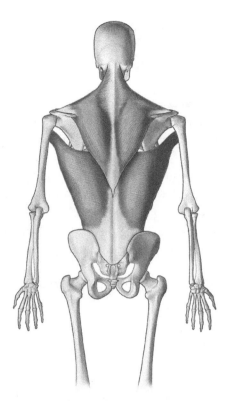

FIGURE 10.4 Latissimus dorsi and trapezius. (*Source/author*: Functional Awareness® and artist Caitlin Duckwall)

      overhead to fifth; you can sense this gliding motion of the inferior scapula gliding slightly up and out.

  f. Downward rotation: The inferior tip of the scapula swings toward the spine and down, which you can sense as you return your arms to your side.

  g. Forward tilt: Once the shoulders elevate a small bit, the scapula can move forward to create the sensation often referred to as hunching.

  h. Return from forward tilt: You can release from the hunching forward position to neutral scapula and this movement is called return from forward tilt.

2. Lift the scapula into elevation quickly. Notice what the neck and head do in relation to this movement. Do you ever experience your shoulders lifting unintentionally while dancing? If this occurs, pause for a moment and allow for a breath to let the scapula release into a rested place on the posterior ribs.

3. Partner B places her hands on the Partner A's scapula as Partner A walks forward. Partner B walks along forward with them, keeping the hands lightly on the shoulder blades. Notice the easy "leaf on the stream" motion of the scapula with the easy swing of the arm structure as Partner A walks.

4. Change positions with your partner.

Exploration: Movements of the Glenohumeral Joint

1. Stand in a comfortable parallel and consider the tripod of balance of the feet and the easeful balance at the AO joint at the top of the spine. Continue standing and move your glenohumeral joint through the following actions.

    a. Flexion: Think of the thumbs leading the action and swing the arm forward.
        i. Do your head and neck want to swing forward as well?
        ii. Move toward ease through the axial skeleton. Think of the wide pectoralis major and latissimus stabilizing the trunk so just the arm structure moves. Allow the head and neck to remain balanced over the spine as the arm moves forward.
    b. Extension: Swing the arm directly behind you. How does your spine react to this action?
    c. Abduction: Bring both arms out to the side up to shoulder height.
    d. Adduction: Let the arms move back down and then cross in front of the body, so your wrists cross.
    e. Medial rotation: Place your left hand on the right upper arm, near the head of the humerus and gently turn the whole arm inward toward the body.
    f. Lateral rotation: Let the left hand remain on the head of the right humerus and gently turn the whole arm outward away from the body.
        i. Move the left hand to the right scapula by touching the tip with the back of your hand or have a partner feel it. Does it move if you turn the arm inward and outward? It should move because the scapula's muscle support attaches to the upper arm.
        ii. Now try to press the shoulder blades down and hold them in place as you move the arm. This movement actually restricts easeful action in the arm.
    g. Circumduction: Move the arm in a large circle, swinging front overhead and then come to the back to complete the circle.

Your Findings and Why They Matter

The scapula is like a leaf on a stream. It glides and moves through the eight motions in response to the actions of the spine, shoulder, and breath. It is not fixed and it can restrict motion if we think we have to force the shoulder blades down the back and secure the scapula with tension. As discovered in Chapter 9 on core support, over-contraction of a muscle group can restrict action and ease in movement rather than support the body.

Exploration: Moving the Arms through a Dance Phrase

1. Choose a familiar sequence of arm movements practiced in dance class.
2. As you begin the phrase with your arms, notice whether your scapula and shoulders have a tendency to elevate or lift toward your ears.
3. Take a moment to envision the large latissimus beginning at the sacrum and fanning out and spiraling around to insert to the front of your upper arm. It is like a broad mainsail of a ship supporting you where you want to navigate the arms for expression.
4. Repeat this same arm phrase from above in two more ways. First lead all the arm movement distally through your fingertips. Next repeat it by leading all the movement from a mid-proximal location, letting the shoulder joint lead all the movement. What do you notice?

Your Findings and Why They Matter

Dancing is a lifelong exploration to discover the balance of the necessary recruitment needed for a movement with the least amount of strain to the system. Discovering the balanced support of the superficial latissimus dorsi and pectoralis major to sustain expressive use of the arm structure is a process of opening through your front without sheering the ribs forward and supporting through the back without pinching the shoulder blades in and down. Whether you lead with the fingertips or move from your shoulder joints, let the shoulder blade glide into action easily with deep central support and see how this affects your dancing.

Mindfulness in Dance Class

There are often four to eight musical counts before each dance exercise as an introduction to the tempo. During the introduction, consider the tripod of balance at the feet, the balance at the AO joint, and the muscular support of the latissimus dorsi and pectoralis major. See if the anatomical images for balance for length and width support the carriage of the arms.

Mindfulness in Daily Life

1. Notice your overall posture when sitting at the computer or in class. If you are in a C-curve, can you feel the glenohumeral joint rolled forward? Is the scapula in elevation or forward tilt? Decide whether this is a useful place to be for the particular activity that you are doing. Is it habit or is it choice?

2. When reaching for something on a shelf, such as a coffee mug, or raising an arm to ask a question, notice where you like to initiate this movement. Try different approaches to the same action of the arms.
3. Notice your arm structure in relation to your sleep position. Does your sleep position support a balanced arm structure? Try using different comfortable alternatives.

Recuperation and Restoring Balance

There are many approaches to mindful practice that elicit recuperation of the body–mind system. Dance requires a great deal of physical exertion and the body often holds tension needed for dancing long after class or rehearsal is over. Time for recuperation and restoration is an important part of any physical activity. A major aspect of rest is sleep! Arranging and then implementing a regular sleep cycle can support a healthy immune system and aid the body in restoring the micro tearing of muscle tissue that is a natural part of building a strong and resilient dancer. The body needs time to repair muscles, regain strength, and replenish energy through sleep. A regular and sufficient sleep pattern should be a priority for all humans, especially for dancers.

This chapter provides three practices for recuperation through imagery and gentle guided movements. These recuperation explorations are helpful to release tension and restore balance. You may also be guided through the explorations by listening to the audio files (www.functionalawareness.org). In addition to the three explorations below, the sequence of mindfulness in breathing in Chapter 9 is a beneficial practice to release tension and return to balance. You may move through these explorations in a chair if lying down on your back with your knees bent in a semi-supine position is not comfortable.

Recuperation Practice 1: A Practice in Neurological Inhibition to Release Tension

Part 1: Right Side

1. Begin by lying down on the floor. Lie down with legs extended and arms extended, by your side, with the palms facing up.

2. Let your body release into the floor. Yield to gravity. Allow the weight of the heels to sense the contact with the earth. Let the weight of the head be taken by the floor. Let your jaw release away from your upper teeth. Bring an easy attention to your breathing.

3. Notice your right leg from the hip to the tips of the toes. Contract the muscles in the right leg and hold on to this contraction. As you are contracting the right leg, notice your lower back. Did it also tense up? Think of releasing the unnecessary tension. Notice your shoulders. Are they tensing to help your legs contract? Think of letting go in the shoulders while continuing to tense the right leg.

4. Release the tension in the right leg now. Gently move the leg around in the hip socket and let go of the contraction.

5. Notice if there is a difference between the right leg that you have just used in contraction and the other leg. Often there is a change in sensation between the two legs, demonstrating a shift in resting length in the muscle spindle that determines the level of tension needed for body action.

6. Make a fist and tense the muscles of the entire right arm from shoulder to fingers. Hold this pose. Notice your neck and see if it is holding tension. Ask yourself to let your neck release. Notice if your jaw has tightened and allow the lower teeth to release away from the upper teeth. Let your breathing support greater ease as you continue to contract the right arm.

7. Open the hand gently and release the tension in the arm. Move the arm in any easy pathway to help release the tension required in the contraction activity.

8. Observe if there is a difference between the right arm and the left.

9. You have now contracted the right arm and right leg. Do you sense any difference between the right and left sides of the body? You probably have discovered some patterns where the body creates tension in your shoulders or jaw, or where you hold your breath or tighten your stomach, no matter what part of the body is asked to contract. These unnecessary tensions deplete energy and contribute to inefficiency in action. As you begin the sequence on the left side, the instructions will ask you to undo unnecessary tension before you begin contracting the body part.

Part 2: Left Side

10. Notice your left leg from the hip to the tips of the toes.

11. This time, before contracting the muscles in the left leg, ask yourself to pause and allow for a breath. Release unwanted tension from the extraneous body parts as you contract the muscles of the left leg. Hold the left leg firmly tense as you continue easy breathing, asking yourself to continue to let go of unnecessary tension.

12. Release the contraction in the left leg now. Gently move the leg around a bit.

13. Notice how both legs feel and gently bend one knee and then the other to bring the feet to the floor into the semi-supine position.

14. Before you make a fist and tense the muscles of the entire left arm, notice your neck and see if it is holding tension. Ask yourself to let the neck release. Notice if your jaw

has tightened and allow the lower teeth to release away from the upper teeth. Notice your breathing and then make the fist with the left hand and contract the muscles in the left arm. Can you sense that you are doing the required action with less overall tension in the body?

15. Open the hand gently and release the tension in the arm. Gently move the arm in an easy pathway to help release the tension. It is a bit like the game of patting your head and rubbing your stomach. In practicing this brain game and inhibiting your habitual responses to do simple actions, the body teaches itself to let go of unwanted tension.

16. Bring both shoulders up by your ears and hold them there. Continue to hold them up as you check in with your breathing. Ask yourself, "Where can I do less, and still hold my shoulders up?" It is a playful exploration.

17. Now release both shoulders down and come to a place of ease in the whole body.

18. Notice general tension level within. Did this change from the beginning of the exploration?

Your Findings and Why They Matter

Recuperation Practice 1 invites you to contract, tense, and hold certain parts of the body for 5 to 10 seconds and then release this tension, enabling the muscles to shift the relaxed resting length of the muscle fibers. The guided practice above heightens awareness of unnecessary tension and invites the body to release this unwarranted muscle contraction.

Mindfulness in Dance Class

After dance class or between dance class and rehearsal, take a moment to recuperate in a semi-supine position. Explore tensing and releasing body parts to activate awareness and sense where you can let go of unnecessary tension.

Mindfulness in Daily Life

When you are a passenger in a car or on public transportation, simply move through the above exploration and practice letting go in other body parts to reduce unnecessary tension. Remember to let the breath support you in the exploration. Recuperation Practice 1 is especially useful when flying on airplanes. It provides a release in tension and allows the body to move without disturbing the folks around you.

Recuperation Practice 2: Rebalancing the Hips, Legs, and Feet

1. Begin in a semi-supine position. Take a moment to release into the floor. Yield to gravity. Notice the weight of the feet and where they make contact with the floor. Notice your breathing without judgment or expectation. Notice inspiration as the air spills in and ask yourself to consider letting go of unnecessary tension on the exhalation.

2. Observe the soles of your feet and how they find contact with the floor. In terms of tripod of balance, are you easily balanced on all three points or do the feet have a different balance at this moment? Do not immediately change; just nonjudgmentally notice how you unconsciously balance the leg.

3. Reconsider the tripod of balance in both feet.

4. Gently extend the right knee and slide the leg straight out along the floor. As you slide, be mindful of maintaining the tripod of balance. Maintain the leg in parallel even after it is completely straight. The body will have a natural tendency to let the leg laterally rotate or turnout.

5. Pause for a moment. Allow for breath. Ask yourself if there are any places in your body where you can let go of any unnecessary tension.

6. Draw the leg into flexion by sliding the foot along the floor. As the leg moves from straight out to bent knee position find the tripod of the foot on the floor. Notice if you favor the outside or inside through inversion or eversion of the foot during this process. Give additional attention to the distal head of the first metatarsal. Observe if this shifts your pathway into a new habit for bending the knee.

7. As you rest the foot back onto the floor with the knee bent, be mindful of the tripod of balance and let all three points of contact have equal weight into the floor.

8. Repeat this sliding out and bending the knee pattern 3 times. This allows for neural repatterning in the body.

9. Repeat this process on the other leg.

Finish the sequence with both knees bent. Let yourself make small adjustments in the body to allow for length in the spine to support the changes in the legs.

Your Findings and Why They Matter

It is common for dancers to have overdeveloped thigh muscles on the more lateral side of the leg and less strength toward the inner thighs. This situation can create an imbalance at the knee and lower leg because there is greater torque on the hinge joint. This quiet restorative process gently brings awareness to habit and creates new patterning for bending and straightening the leg.

Mindfulness in Dance Class

Recuperation Practice 2 aids to restore balance in the musculature of the legs after the rigorous demands of dance class. It is restful and an alternative to foam rolling as an approach to release thigh tension before or following dance class.

Mindfulness in Daily Life

When you are sitting in a chair, notice your habitual positions for the feet and legs. There is no judgment in this activity, just an opportunity to become aware of how your feet and legs prefer to support you while sitting. Consider repositioning the feet through the tripod of balance to recuperate from any asymmetrical patterns you notice.

Recuperation Practice 3: Releasing Tension in the Arms (Snow Angel)

1. Begin on the floor in a semi-supine position. Rest with arms extended with the palms facing up.
2. Notice your breathing. Notice inspiration as the air spills in and ask yourself to consider letting go of unnecessary tension on the exhalation.
3. Let the lips remain together as the teeth rest slightly apart to release unnecessary tension in the temporomandibular joint.
4. Think of an image of water spilling from your neck, down both arms, and all the way through your fingertips.
5. Now give the water a color. In the instructions that follow, think of the color like finger paint, and let your fingers lead the actions of the arms. This movement is called distal initiation of the arm.
6. With the palms facing up, move both arms away from your hips toward your head. At first move both arms like a butterfly opening its wings. Move just 2 or 3 inches and rest.
7. Flip the hands to face down, slowly leading with the fingertips, and rest again.
8. Let the fingertips lead the action; turn the palms to face up again and travel several more inches, opening the butterfly wings so the arms are outstretched forming a T-shape with the body.
9. Flip the hands to face down slowly and rest.
10. Flip the palms to face up again and travel several more inches so the arms form a high V-shape above shoulder height. Let your butterfly wings fully open.
11. Pause to allow for mindfulness of a few cycles of breath, and let your jaw release away from the upper teeth.
12. Return to close the butterfly wings. When moving the arms back down toward your thighs, the hands are facing palms down during the descent.
13. With the fingertips leading the action distally, travel to lower the arms to the T-shape and then pause and flip the palms up.
14. Turn the hands one last time to face down and make your descent to close the butterfly wings and rest the arms by your side.
15. Turn the palms up to finish the movement.
16. Pause and rest to allow for a moment to release unwanted tension.

Your Findings and Why They Matter

It is not unusual for dancers to experience tension in the shoulders, neck, and jaw. This activity has the nickname of the snow angel because if feels like a slower, mindful version of that activity we perform when falling on our backs in the snow. It should also have that childlike sense of play and fun. The activity naturally engages the muscles of the rotator cuff while allowing the body to release from tension that is often the residue of habitual action. Let yourself enjoy the movement.

Mindfulness in Dance Class

Recuperation Practice 3 can be done standing along a wall or lying down on the floor before class to open the arm structure and release tension to enhance expressivity of the arms during class.

Mindfulness in Daily Life

When going to reach for something on a shelf, such as a coffee mug, or to raise an arm to ask a question, notice where you like to initiate this movement. Play with different approaches to the same action of the arms. Initiate it distally from your fingertips. Initiate it more proximally from your shoulders first. Explore the differences.

Conclusion

Gathering the Knowledge to Move Forward

The previous chapters offer a series of movement explorations that engage the readers in anatomical body mapping and encourage them to experiment, explore, and discover things about their own body and their habitual choices in movement. The beauty of artistic expression is within the myriad of ways humans are capable of moving and communicating through movement and dance. Functional Awareness® investigates the ways in which dancers can embody their artistry and expression while maintaining a healthy body. It is important for the body to release unnecessary tension as it often impedes performance and can cause pain. Once released, the mover has the ability to recruit the required muscles for dynamic alignment. It is essential to recuperate; this can be done through moving toward balance. Through anecdotal stories and anatomical explanations of the body, the reader learns that no one is symmetrical or perfectly balanced. Yet everyone has the ability to make changes and move with ease.

At the closing of each Functional Awareness® workshop or course, we have a final practice at the end of each session called 'beach glass and shells.' It is a time to gather thoughts of what you have experienced.

The Story: *Beach Glass and Shells*

Both authors have spent countless hours together on the beaches of New York, Florida, Delaware, and Maryland. When walking along the beach we might focus our eyes out onto the horizon. Then we gaze along the beach. We scan for objects resting in the sand. We become curious about a shell or horseshoe crab. Occasionally there is something that captivates our attention and engages us enough to pick it up, spend more time with it, and put it in our pocket as a keepsake to remember the day or the moment. Perhaps it is a glimmering piece of smooth sea-foam-colored beach glass; or perhaps it is an unusually shaped shell. Pick it up, put in the pocket, and save it to examine further at another time or leave it in the pocket to just feel later in the day and remember.

During your journey of reading the book, what discoveries or ideas engaged you? What questions or further inquiries bubbled up during the course of chapters? What are

FIGURE 12.1 Beach Glass and Shells (*Source/author*: With permission from Jim Burger Photography)

those morsels of information or experiences that you've picked up along the way? What are your shells or pieces of beach glass?

Writing Exploration: Beach Glass and Shells

1. What concepts during the readings call for further play and exploration?
    a. Take a moment to reflect on what concepts, imagery, or movement explorations might be a piece of beach glass for you.
    b. Glance back through the book and find one thing in each chapter to record as your beach glass or shell.
        i. It can be something you question and wish to investigate further.
        ii. It can be something that engaged you and you want to put into practice.

Further Steps: Putting It into Practice

Continue to bring awareness to your habitual patterns of movement and how they affect your dancing and your everyday life. Continue to seek the end-ranges of movement and explore the reaches of your artistry. Enjoy the energetic satisfaction of exertion and also allow time for recuperation. Recuperation can be as simple as a moment's pause, to allow for breath to release, recruit, and recover. Balance can be a moment's consideration of the tripod at the feet to move toward balance in the body. We invite you to utilize Functional Awareness®: Anatomy in Action and the shells and beach glass you've collected thus far as tools for discovery, exploration, and change.

Glossary of Terms
in Human Anatomy

PLANES OF THE BODY

transverse or horizontal: plane divides the body into upper and lower parts, superior and inferior.

median or mid-sagittal: plane divides the body in right and left halves

coronal or frontal: plane divides the body into front and back, or anterior and posterior parts.

ANATOMICAL TERMS OF REFERENCE

anterior: indicates the front of the body.

posterior: indicates the back portion of the body.

superior: indicates a position on the body above the point of reference.

inferior: indicates a position on the body below the point of reference.

proximal: indicates closer to the trunk, or joint of reference.

distal: indicates farther from the trunk or joint of reference.

flexion: indicates movement in the sagittal plane that takes the body forward.

extension: indicates movement in the sagittal plane that takes the body backward.

ipsilateral: indicates movement on the same side of the body.

contralateral: indicates movement on opposite sides of the body.

abduction: indicates movement away from the median plane.

adduction: indicates movement towards the median plane

medial rotation: indicates movement in transverse plane moving inward.

lateral rotation: indicates movement in the transverse (horizontal) plane moving outward.

superficial: designates position on the exterior part of the body.

deep: designates a position on an internal part of the body.

supination: indicates movement with the palm of the hand facing forward (as if it could hold a bowl of soup).

pronation: indicates a movement with the palm of the hand facing backward.

Bibliography

Bartenieff, Imgard. *Body Movement: Coping with the Environment*. New York: Routledge, 1980.

Brennan, Richard. *The Alexander Technique Workbook*. Boston: Collins & Brown, 2011.

Calais-Germain, Blandine. *Anatomy of Breathing*. Seattle: Eastland Press, Inc., 2006.

Cho, E. "Integration of Body and Mind Through Kinesthetic Imagery: Nancy Topf's Repatterning Technique in Modern Dance Training and Creative Process." PhD diss., New York University, 1998.

Dixon, Emma. "The mind/body connection and the practice of classical ballet." *Research in Dance Education* 6 (2005): 75–96.

Dowd, Irene. *Taking Root to Fly*. New York: Irene Dowd, 1990.

Earls, James. *Born to Walk: Myofascial Efficiency and the Body in Movement*. Berkeley, Calif.: North Atlantic Books, 2014.

Franklin, Eric. *Conditioning for Dance*. Champaign, Ill.: Human Kinetics, 2004.

Hackney, Peggy. *Making Connections: Total Body Integration Through Bartenieff Fundamentals*. New York: Taylor & Francis, 2002.

Hargrove, Todd. *A Guide to Better Movement*. Seattle: Better Movement, 2014.

H'Doubler, Margaret. *Dance, a Creative Art Experience*. Madison: University of Wisconsin Press, 1998.

Huxley, Michael. "F. Matthias Alexander and Mabel Elsworth Todd: proximities, practices and the psycho-physical." *Journal of Dance & Somatic Practices* 3 (2012): 25–42.

Koch, Liz. *The Psoas Book*, 30th Anniversary Revised Edition. Felton, Calif.: Core Awareness, 2012. http://www.coreawareness.com.

Leibowitz, Judy. *Dare to Be Wrong: The Teaching of Judy Leibowitz*. New York: American Center for the Alexander Technique, 2007.

Matt, Pamela. "Ideokinesis: Integrating the science and somatics of dance." *Kinesiology and Medicine for Dance* 14 (1992): 69–77.

Nettl-Fiol, Vanier. *Dance and the Alexander Technique: Exploring the Missing Link*. Champaign-Urbana: University of Illinois Press, 2011.

Sajko, Sandy, and Stuber Kent. "Psoas Major: A case report and review of its anatomy, biomechanics, and clinical implications." *The Journal of the Canadien Chiropractic Organization* 53, no. 4 (December 2009): 311–318.

Todd, Mabel Elsworth. *The Thinking Body*. Brooklyn, N.Y.: Dance Horizons, 1937.

Further Readings

CHAPTER 3
Leibowitz, Judy. *Dare to Be Wrong: The Teaching of Judy Leibowitz*. New York: American Center for the Alexander Technique, 2007.

CHAPTER 5
Hackney, Peggy. *Making Connections: Total Body Integration Through Bartenieff Fundamentals*. New York: Taylor & Francis, 2002.

CHAPTER 6
Franklin, Eric. *Conditioning for Dance*. Champaign, Ill.: Human Kinetics, 2004.

CHAPTER 7
Earls, James. *Born to Walk: Myofascial Efficiency and the Body in Movement*. Berkeley, Calif.: North Atlantic Books, 2014.

CHAPTER 8
Calais-Germain, Blandine. *Anatomy of Breathing*. Seattle: Eastland Press, 2006.

CHAPTER 9
Bartenieff, Imgard. *Body Movement: Coping with the Environment*. New York: Routledge, 1980.
Koch, Liz. *The Psoas Book*, 30th Anniversary Revised Edition. Felton, Calif.: Core Awareness, 2012. http://www.coreawareness.com.

Index

Functional Awareness

Functional Awareness

Anatomy in Action for Dancers

Nancy Romita

AND

Allegra Romita

OXFORD
UNIVERSITY PRESS

OXFORD
UNIVERSITY PRESS

Oxford University Press is a department of the University of Oxford. It furthers
the University's objective of excellence in research, scholarship, and education
by publishing worldwide. Oxford is a registered trade mark of Oxford University
Press in the UK and certain other countries.

Published in the United States of America by Oxford University Press
198 Madison Avenue, New York, NY 10016, United States of America.

Library of Congress Cataloging-in-Publication Data
Names: Romita, Nancy, author. | Romita, Allegra, author.
Title: Functional awareness : anatomy in action for dancers / Nancy Romita and Allegra Romita.
Description: New York : Oxford University Press, 2016. | Includes bibliographical references and index.
Identifiers: LCCN 2015051067 | ISBN 9780190498139 (hardback)
Subjects: LCSH: Dance—Physiological aspects. | Dancers—Training of. | Mind and body. | Muscular sense. |
BISAC: MUSIC / Genres & Styles / Dance. | MUSIC / Genres & Styles / Ballet.
Classification: LCC RC1220.D35 R66 2016 | DDC 617.1/0275—dc23 LC record available at
http://lccn.loc.gov/2015051067
9780190498139 cloth
9780190498146 paper
9780190498153 updf
9780190498160 epub

Contents

Homage

Nancy and Allegra wish to pay homage to their somatic and embodied anatomy teachers, guides, and predecessors. It is by no means a complete list, but it identifies key influences in our current research.

Nancy owes gratitude to teacher/mentor Martha Myers and her visionary work to integrate somatic exploration with dance training at Nancy's alma mater, Connecticut College. In the 1970s Martha introduced Nancy to somatic work with Irene Dowd at Connecticut College as well as Bartenieff Fundamentals, Feldenkrais Method, Alexander Technique with Missy Vineyard, and Dance Movement Therapy with Linni Silberman and Elaine Siegel at the American Dance Festival. These early experiences in somatic education led Nancy on a lifelong exploration to support performing artists in discovering easeful use and integrated movement function. In addition, Nancy gives profound thanks to the American Center for the Alexander Technique, particularly her primary trainers, Judy Leibowitz, Barbara Kent, and Debbie Caplan, for providing a pathway to the psychophysical philosophies and principles she embodies and conveys daily through the work of FM Alexander. Alexander's approach to the relationship between structure, function, and use has deeply informed Nancy's somatic investigations.

Allegra pays homage to her coauthor and mother. She is a thoughtful and supportive parent, business partner, artist, mentor, friend, and somatic teacher. Allegra is grateful to her formative dance teachers at Towson University and University of Michigan. She thanks Sid McNairy, Amy Chavasse, and Ossi Raveh, who encouraged the yogi and the teacher within, and Ananda Apfelbaum for an approach to hands-on healing through Thai Massage Sacred Bodywork. She appreciates those who influenced her understanding of embodied anatomy: Amy Matthews, Marika Molnar, Khita Whyatt, Cheryl Clark, and John Chanik. In addition, Allegra is grateful to those who ignited her interest in dance education, writing, and curriculum design at NYU, particularly Dr. Susan Koff, Pat Cohen, Deborah Damast, and Claire Porter.

Both authors thank their predecessors in somatic literature, including FM Alexander, Irmgard Bartenieff, Mabel Todd, Margaret H'Doubler, Irene Dowd, Glenna Batson, Bonnie Bainbridge Cohen, Eric Franklin, Peggy Hackney, and Martha Eddy to name a few.

Finally, Nancy thanks her coauthor, collaborator, colleague, and daughter, Allegra. Her inspiring and innovative thinking on the relationship of biomechanical function and the artistry of movement is a gift. This journey is not possible without her partnership and coauthorship.

In the collective professional experience of training people in somatic-based practices, the authors have had vast and varied influences on their work. After many years of applying functional movement theory into practice, it is hard to distinguish the original sources of many of the practices and stories implemented. This book contains a bibliography to acknowledge the mentors, teachers, and literature that influenced this current path of integrated knowledge. If the authors are aware of the origin of a specific story or anatomical information, it will be referenced. There is a rich body of literature in embodied anatomy that precedes *Functional Awareness*. A suggested reading on each topic is provided at the end of the book to encourage readers to continue their investigations in embodied practices.

Acknowledgments

The authors thank the many people who supported this project by their generous gift of their time and talents. The authors owe a supreme debt of gratitude to Betsy Winship, our guide to editing and book publishing in the early stages of preparing the manuscript for submission. We thank Lisbeth Redfield, for her early belief, encouragement, and support for this book. We thank the anonymous readers for Oxford University Press. Their thoughtful comments helped shape and clarify our writing. Also we thank Norm Hirschy for his support and stewardship of the manuscript at Oxford University Press.

Many thanks to Jim Burger and JP Burger Photography for his artistic talents and photographs, Hollis McCracken for her pencil drawings, and Caitlin Duckwall for her artistic rendering of the FA® anatomical images.

In addition, we appreciate and thank Dr. Susan Kirchner at Towson University for encouraging us to deepen the research in somatic principles as they relate to the practice of dance performance. We thank Dana J. Martin, Wendy Salkind, and Jerri-Lynn Pilarski for their support as readers and generously contributing their thoughts and feedback.

Finally, both authors thank Vic Romita, loving husband and father, for his undying enthusiasm and support for all artistic endeavors partaken.

Introduction

Functional Awareness: Anatomy in Action for Dancers is an approach to understanding the body and how it functions through movement explorations in experiential anatomy with applications to dance training. It connects the scientific with the somatic. It connects anatomy with artistry. Applied practice of the Functional Awareness® principles enables one to efficiently recruit muscle actions to improve dance technique, release unnecessary muscular tension, and develop a balance between exertion and recuperation.

The book is a combination of two distinctive dance artists and their varied somatic backgrounds combining to form a connected process that stands as its own somatic approach. Allegra brings her background in Thai massage, yoga, dance performance for social change, movement science, and Laban Movement Analysis. Nancy's background in professional performance and choreography, Alexander Technique and functional anatomy adds additional perspectives to the development of this somatic approach. Together, over 35,000 hours of teaching, training, movement, and academic research supports the development of the principles in Functional Awareness®.

Similar to the tradition in modern dance where dancers are constantly inventing and reinventing new forms of movement expression, Functional Awareness® stands on the shoulders of the giants in embodied anatomy that precede us in order to integrate and create another lens on how humans move and how movement choices affect dance training and daily life.

Functional Awareness® is a movement philosophy based in the principles of efficient movement function, a lively curiosity to invite new body understanding, and a practice of nonjudgmental noticing, in order to appreciate the unique gifts in each dancing body. The reader is invited to apply the concepts in each chapter to dance skills as well as during quotidian or everyday tasks. Discovering daily mindfulness of body choices develops a profound deepening of one's dance artistry, while providing recuperation from the end-range actions of the rigorous requirements of dance.

This book is written for all dance enthusiasts interested in learning more about their body and offers tools to improve dance training. The book is for dancers, movement educators, professional dancers, and somatic practitioners. It is not an anatomy text, but rather a book introducing some anatomical concepts to provide cognitive context for sensory explorations. Basic principles of anatomy are discussed to enhance understanding of how the body can move with less stress and greater ease. The movement explorations and anatomical information establish a platform for exploration, discovery, and discussion. The material accumulates to create building blocks for mindful patterns in daily movement.

In dance we constantly seek the end-ranges of movement and often achieve spectacular artistic results. At times, it also results in a cost to our physical structure. It is our quest to develop strategies for stability and recovery, to discover efficiency of body action, and to provide simple, accessible tools so people can move for a lifetime with ease and grace.

Relationship of Habit to Dance Training

Functional Awareness® (FA) is a practical somatic method that provides a series of explorations in experiential anatomy to enhance our understanding of movement function, facilitate ease in body action, and improve dynamic alignment for dancing. FA investigates anatomical features of the skeletal structure, the muscular structure, and the myofascial tissue to help sustain elasticity, flexibility, and efficiency in movement, using the principles of release, recruit, and restore. *Functional Awareness: Anatomy in Action for Dancers* applies cognitive anatomical knowledge with a kinesthetic or sensory experience to deepen one's investigations to improve dynamic alignment and dance technique. It integrates anatomical theory, dance practice, and daily living, encouraging more choices of movement strategies. Most books on dance training seek to improve the dancer's actions in the training environment of the classroom. This book addresses studio practice and also presents mindful practices during daily life. These practices within daily life can have a profound impact on improving dance skills and provide tools to move with greater ease for a lifetime. Dance students using the FA training return after many years to express that the practices learned through this approach are still a part of their daily life, performing life, and teaching practice. This work seeks to create an embodiment of anatomy to facilitate ease and efficacy in movement.

Many people experience tension or pain and assume this is something that "just happens" to them. It is as if the body is a separate entity. People think of joint and body pain as being like a cold virus: we just pick it up from somewhere. Often there is no one particular event to precipitate the discomfort. Most muscular discomfort actually arises from something we do or more often it is the way in which we do it. If the action is repeated with frequency, it creates wear on the system and leads to pain and discomfort over time. In a sense, people "practice" discomfort through unconscious posture and movement habits. The following is an old joke to illustrate this point.

The Story: How Your Suit Fits

A woman has taken her pantsuit to be fixed and altered by a tailor. She tries on the outfit to be sure the alternations are correct. As she tries on the pants, she notices the leg lengths appear different.

The tailor is not interested in doing more work so he just adjusts her hip a bit and now the legs look even. The woman adjusts and decides she can live with this. The woman now tries on the jacket and discovers one sleeve is too long and also the darts make the jacket hard to button in the front. The tailor just says, "Look if you just make this little adjustment in your shoulders, it will fit perfectly."

The woman actually buys into this sales pitch, makes the adjustment, and walks out of the store. As she is walking out of the store and down the street two people are coming at her from the opposite direction. One says, "Look at that poor woman." "Yes," the other one says, "Doesn't her suit fit perfectly!"

People make subtle or larger adjustments in life and these adjustments become habits that are unconscious. Over time they begin to take a physical toll on our system. This toll is exhibited in tension, pain, stiffness, or rigidity of movement. The good news: It is possible to shift posture and movement habits and discover more ease and less tension in the body. Here are three simple approaches:

1. Become more aware of your personal movement habits.
2. Learn a basic understanding about how the musculoskeletal system functions, and how this affects body action.
3. Practice new skills to improve movement function and dynamic alignment.

Exploration: Becoming More Aware of Our Movement Habits

Try this experiment:

1. Clasp your hands together with all the fingers crossed.
2. Notice which thumb is on top. Is it your writing hand or your non-dominant hand?
3. Open your hands and close them quickly and unconsciously. Does the same arrangement in your thumbs and hand arise?
4. Now release your hands and reweave your fingers to place the other thumb on top. How comfortable or uncomfortable is this? Does it take a little more time for your brain to tell your body how to place your hands in this way?

Try the same activity with your arms crossed.

1. Fold your arms.
2. Notice which arm is on the top. Is this the same arm as the thumb earlier?

3.   Drop your arms by your side and now raise your arms to fold the arms with the opposite forearm on top. How does this feel? Often we have a preferred manner in which
we fold our arms and the other way feels a bit peculiar.

Try the same activity with legs crossed.

1.   Cross your legs or your ankles if that is more familiar to you.
2.   Notice which leg is on the top. Is this the same leg as the arm earlier?
3.   Uncross the legs and then try the other side. How does this feel?

In facilitating this activity for over thirty years to thousands of people, we realize
that these habits are not systemic and have no pattern in regard to dominant hand or
genetic proclivity. They are merely "how your suit fits" or how you have made a habitual
accommodation over time.

Some habits are compulsory and very positive, such as brushing our teeth or auto-
matically moving the foot to the break pad when a light turns yellow and then red. Some
habits are unnecessary.

Unconscious habits with posture can compromise body balance, place unnecessary
stress on the system, and lead to discomfort and pain. Improving your range of choices
for movement develops a more resilient neuromuscular system.

Your Findings and Why They Matter

My grandmother was born in 1900. Using life insurance statistics, the average life expec-
tancy for a woman born in 1900 in America (married and a nonsmoker) was age fifty.
Life expectancy for a woman born in 2000 who is married and does not smoke is now
ninety!

We only get one skeletal system for a lifetime. If my grandmother had a little ar-
thritis or chronic discomfort as she started to grow older, she had to deal with this only
until age fifty (on average). We now live almost twice as long on average! It behooves us
to know more about how our unconscious habits affect our musculoskeletal system and
how this unconsciously contributes to chronic discomfort or worse. More importantly,
we can prevent and change patterns of movement to alleviate pressure on the system
through some techniques and practices in awareness.

Chronic unconscious misuse of the body leads to chronic discomfort or pain.
A subtle habit can have a profound impact over time. Folding your hands does not have a
large impact on your neuromuscular system, but crossing your arms often leads to many
other accommodations so the body becomes imbalanced.

Crossing one leg far more often than the other can lead to an imbalance in the hips.
If your legs are crossed right now, notice if you have more weight on one hip. You may
want to check this out while you are driving. Are you always leaning slightly into one
hip? This constant small imbalance creates instability in the lower back and pelvis, and

this can lead to pain or discomfort over time. How you move through daily action affects your whole health.

The Anatomy: The Skeletal Structure

Our skeletal structure is the scaffolding that supports the other body systems. To have a framework of understanding about the body, it is helpful to be able to name and identify basic elements of the skeletal structure. (See Figure 1.1.)

There are seven vertebrae in the neck or cervical spine. The first cervical vertebra is called the atlas. Just as the Greek god Atlas held up the entire world, this first cervical vertebra holds up our world of ideas and thinking. The atlas or C1 vertebra articulates with the skull at the occiput. The top of our spine does not end at the base of the skull. The first vertebra or atlas meets the skull at the occiput. (See Figure1.2.)

The atlas is the pivot point to nod yes. If we begin the action at this place, minimal impact is made on the spine. If we habitually nod to look down at our computer or phone with the vertebra farther down the spine, the large muscle structures of the back have to do far more work. This can lead to muscle fatigue and pain.

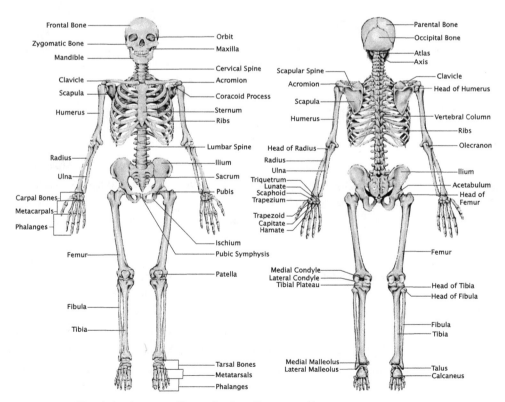

FIGURE 1.1 The skeletal system. (*Source/author*: Shutterstock)

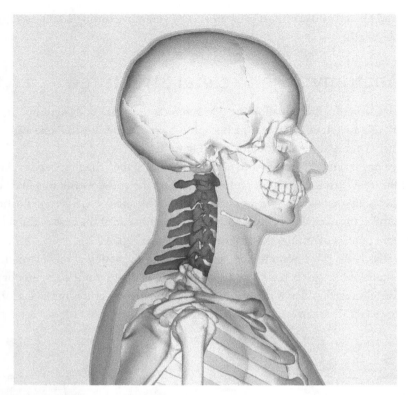

FIGURE 1.2 The skull and cervical spine. (*Source/author*: http://en.wikipedia.org/wiki/Cervical_vertebrae#mediaviewer/File:Cervical_vertebrae_lateral2.png; *Gray's Anatomy* in the public domain)

Why Is This Structural Understanding of the Body Useful to Know?

Unconscious movement habits promote imbalance in the skeletal structure. It can be detrimental to the body, leading to pain and accelerated joint deterioration. How we stand or sit or hold our head affects overall function. Our head is the very top or most superior portion of the skeletal system. How it is poised on the spine has a very potent impact on how we move.

The adult head weighs ten to twelve pounds on average. How this structure is balanced at the top of our spine affects the rest of the musculoskeletal system in significant ways. The amount of physical exertion needed to support the head is minimal if it remains poised with the ears aligned over the shoulders and hips, as shown in the left image in Figure 1.3. If we have a habit of jutting our face forward to see the computer screen or to read this book, the amount of physical stress and energy can be up to three times greater on the system. This action to jut the face forward creates wear and tear on the vertebrae and fatigue and overuse symptoms in the muscle structure. This effect can be observed in the middle and right-hand images in Figure 1.3.

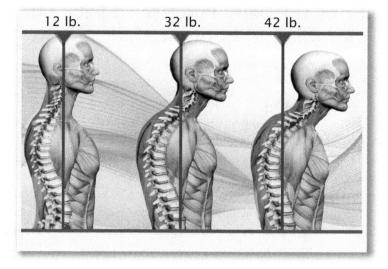

FIGURE 1.3 Habitual head posture's effect on the spine. (*Source/author*: With permission from Erik Dalton)

Exploration: Improve Your Skills for Functional Awareness® in Action

Notice the relationship of your head to your neck and spine in daily activities.

1. What happens to your neck and head when you slump, when you work at the computer? Does your head pull the face forward? This position actually tips the weight of the skull down onto the cervical vertebrae.
2. Do you like to bring your food up to your face, or do you bring your face to your food by pulling your face forward to the fork? This action of face forward compresses the cervical vertebrae.

How This Positioning Affects Dance Technique Training

In dynamic alignment, if your head is not aligned over the spine, this positioning creates instability. An example of how this can affect your dancing is a lack of reliability for a clear turning axis. It is harder to balance and it is more difficult to execute multiple turns reliably. Your ability for vertical height in jumping is compromised as well. It is very difficult for the body to suddenly align the head during a dance phrase if most of the day you are craning the head forward while looking at your cell phone or computer screen.

Suggestions for Daily Practice to Facilitate a Shift in Habit and Improve Dance Skills

For all daily practices, follow a simple three-step process:

1. Discover how your "suit fits." What are your habits for head balance, arm cross, and leg cross? None of this is wrong or bad posture. It is merely an unconscious pattern that can contribute to imbalance in the system. We all have habits of asymmetry. It is awareness of these habits and choosing when they are necessary that enhances postural health and efficiency of movement.
2. Consider letting yourself move out of habit and into a state of curiosity about balancing the body differently. Play with letting your eyes gaze the horizon to rebalance where the first vertebra of the atlas meets the skull or occiput (the AO joint).
3. Keep a movement journal to record your findings. This journal can help you notice patterns over time.

Skeletal Center of Gravity

Moving out of Habit and into a Balanced Standing Posture

Standing is a daily activity that can promote balance, or it can systemically compromise the spine and be a source for discomfort and pain. Habit plays an important role in the choices one makes for standing. The principles for easeful standing involve moving toward symmetry in the body. No one is completely symmetrical. It is important to move the body toward symmetry and balance so you exert equal force on your structure. Unequal force over time compromises the body structure and weakens joints and muscles.

The Story: *My Three Sons*

One student, John, a tall gentleman in his late forties, came to see me because he had severe and chronic back pain in his lower back or lumbar area. He had tried surgery involving spinal fusion. This surgery provided a temporary relief, but over time his pain returned.

Figure 2.1 shows what John's posture looked like.

I explained to John that, as young babies and toddlers, our standing balance is well organized with little unnecessary effort. Over time we start to accommodate to our surrounding environment. For example, tall people may slouch down to accommodate to a chair that is too small. As people move into the teenage years there are psychophysical accommodations that are often made unconsciously. A teenager may think that he is too tall and intentionally slouch. Someone else may feel too short and try to lift his chin to appear taller.

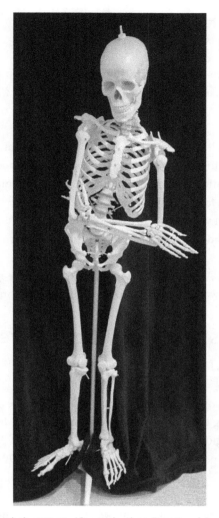

FIGURE 2.1 John's posture. (*Source/author*: Functional Awareness®)

During this explanation to John, he exclaims, "Oh! I know where this habit of standing comes from! When I was a boy there was a TV show called My Three Sons, *and at the start of every show they had the three sons standing there with one son tapping his foot during the theme song. The teenage boy, Rob, was so cool on that show. I remember when I was ten, I said to myself 'I am going to be cool and stand like Rob'!"*

Most people do not have an "aha" moment as to when they begin to take on a habit. People do have the capacity to observe current patterns and begin to think consciously about how our environment does affect stance in life. When the brain thinks about the principles of balance, the body's muscle system responds. Using the tools of Functional Awareness®, John was able to shift his postural habits, relieve his chronic back pain, and feel in more control of his body actions.

Exploration: How Does Your Suit Fit While Standing?

There are two key habits to observe in standing. How are your feet connecting to the earth? Where is your head in relation to the rest of your spine? Try the following experiment:

1. Close your eyes while facing a mirror. Stand for a moment as if you were waiting in line at the grocery store. Just settle into the habit that feels comfortable in standing.
2. Open your eyes. Notice if you are standing on leg more than the other.
3. Notice if one foot is farther out ahead than the other.
4. Place your palms on your hips and notice if one hip bone is rotated forward.
5. Now stand with a side view to the mirror and close your eyes to find your habit in standing.
6. Open yours to eyes. Are your head and face forward of the rest of your spine?
7. Are you leaning forward on the balls of your feet or back on your heels?

Your Findings and Why They Matter

Answer these questions for yourself:

1. While dancing, do you favor using one leg to turn over the other?
2. Do you have one leg that you prefer as your standing leg? For example, does one leg support you in adagio movement more reliably?
3. Do you prefer fifth position with the right leg in front? Or how about the left leg in front? Do these feel the same?

Recognizing your standing habit is the gateway to understanding movement efficiency in dance. It is a bit easier to observe habitual idiosyncrasies while standing still. If you wear out your left shoe more than your right shoe, this indicates that you habitually place more weight on that foot as well as that hip, creating a pattern to "wear out" that side of your body at a faster rate than the other side. You can prevent this with a simple reminder to move toward balanced standing.

The Anatomy: Skeletal Center of Gravity

Your skeletal system can balance in standing with minimal stress to the neuromuscular system. Unconscious habits of imbalance cause chronic strain that lead to discomfort and pain.

If you are standing with your center of gravity (COG) aligned, as shown in Figure 2.2, the body musculature is balanced and there is little stress on the system.

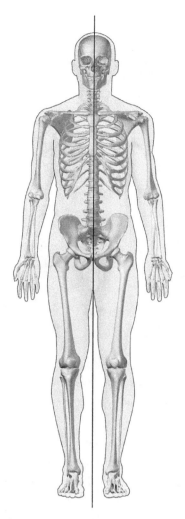

FIGURE 2.2 Skeleton COG front view. (*Source/author*: Functional Awareness® and Caitlin Duckwall)

Many people are like John and develop unconscious poor posture habits, moving the center of gravity into imbalance. When the system is not balanced through the COG, muscles overwork and uneven skeletal alignment places unnecessary pressure on the vertebrae and joints.

Look at the line down the middle in the front view of the skeleton depicted in Figure 2.2. This line is often referred to as the plumb line of balance for the body in the sagittal plane. The mid-sagittal plane equally divides the body into right and left halves. If you stand in the "cool Rob" from *My Three Sons* position, throwing the weight into one hip more than the other, you create an imbalance in the neuromuscular system.

Look at the person in balanced standing on the grid in Figure 2.3. The line identifying the frontal or coronal plane separates the body into front and back halves. If the face

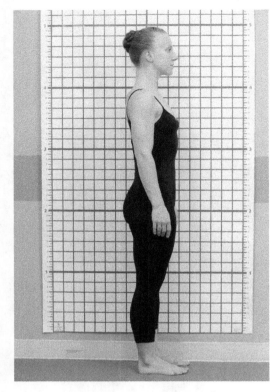

FIGURE 2.3 Balanced standing. (*Source/author*: With permission from Jim Burger Photography)

juts forward, as mentioned in the previous chapter, the COG moves, creating an imbalance in the neuromuscular system that can lead to muscle fatigue and discomfort. If your weight is falling back on your heels, the rest of your system starts to "'grab'" or hold on to muscle tension to prevent you from falling backward. Leaning too far forward on the balls of the feet or too far back on the heels can be common causes for back pain. If you are leaning forward with more weight on the balls of your feet, so the COG line falls through your kneecaps (patella), unnecessary pressure is placed on the pelvis, hips, and particularly knees.

Importance of the Balance at Your Feet

Where your balance is at your feet is important to discover in order to maintain dynamic alignment. Many people think of the foot as one lump that fits into a shoe. The foot is actually composed of twenty-six articulating bones. In addition, the foot contains a couple of sesamoid bones (bones embedded in tendons) to provide shock absorption or cushion for the ball of the foot. With twenty-six articulating bones and thirty-one joints, we have many choices for how we stand on our feet.

Easeful balance is often achieved if the foot is resting evenly at three points of contact. These points of contact are called the tripod of balance. Anatomically speaking, these

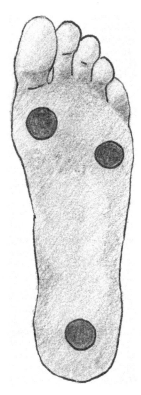

FIGURE 2.4 Tripod of the foot. (*Source/Artist*: With permission from Hollis McCracken)

balance points are the distal head of distal first metatarsal, the distal head of the fifth meta-tarsal, and the anterior calcaneus or between the lateral and medial malleoli. Figure 2.4 helps to visualize these points of balance on the bottom of the foot. If the feet are balanced and the head is poised through the COG (demonstrated in Figure 2.3), the body often "corrects" many posture imbalances unconsciously when the key points for balance at the feet and the head are well organized.

Exploration: Getting out of Habit for the Feet

This simple exploration applies gentle pressure to the soles of the feet. In this way the habitual stance for balance becomes unhabituated. It then releases habitual tension and allows the foot to discover the tripod of balance with ease.

Part 1
1. Take one or two athletic socks and roll them up in a ball.
2. Stand with your feet in parallel, with equal weight on both feet. The feet about hip distance apart.

3. Place the sock under the right foot so it is about center on the arch.
4. Now move both feet forward onto your toes and lift the heels off the floor. Then rock back onto the heels, rolling gently through the pressure of the sock. Repeat this several times.
5. Take the sock out from under the right foot. See if the right foot feels different from the left. For some it may feel odd, for others it may feel more stable, and for some it does not feel very different. All these experiences are valid and helpful in terms of letting the body move out of habit and into awareness.

Part 2

1. Repeat Steps 1 to 5 with the sock under the left foot.
2. Notice if there is a change.

Here are some other helpful guidelines to easeful balance in standing:

1. Place your feet equally on the three points of contact called the tripod of balance.
2. Let your eyes gaze at a point on the horizon because this often helps to balance the head at the atlanto-occipital joint mentioned in the first chapter.
3. Align your ears, shoulders, hips, and ankles while standing.

Mindfulness in Dance Class

1. When you are watching the teacher demonstrate an exercise, notice your habitual patterns for standing. Are you leaning into a hip? Is it almost always the same hip? Is one foot always out ahead of the other with the hip also rotated forward? These habits cause muscular imbalances that make dynamic alignment more difficult during the actual exercises of dance practice and performance.
2. If you notice one foot ahead of the other or more weight on one leg, practice the following: pause and allow for a breath, gently shift the feet to discover the tripod of balance, let your focus gaze out at eye level, and let the rest sort itself out. It is not about attaining a position; it is about making a choice to move in the direction of balance.

Over the years students have asked for some helpful information on how to stand for long periods of time, as the body seeks a balanced reciprocity between exertion and recuperation. To prevent fatigue the body appreciates small, frequent adjustments to maintain a dynamic alignment.

Tips for Standing for Long Periods of Time

1. Let your eyes focus out to the horizon to let your head poise on your spine and find the tripod of balance for your feet.

2. Gently shift your weight through the tripod by subtly moving toward the right front big toe, and then to the outside of the foot, moving back to the weight on the right heel. Then shift the weight to the left heel and around to the outside of the left foot and onto the big toe of the left foot. This slow, gentle, circular shift of weight ensures a lively dialogue between your body habit for standing and dynamic alignment.

Mindfulness in Daily Life

1. When you are waiting in a line at the grocery store, notice your habitual patterns for standing.
2. Pause and allow for a breath. Let your eyes gaze the horizon. Discover the tripod of balance at your feet, and let the rest sort itself out.

Gentle reminder: There is no wrong way to stand. The body can move in many ways. You are merely considering the role that unconscious habit has in contributing to imbalances in your structure and making some choices to recuperate from those stresses by moving out of habit and into awareness.

3

Anatomical and Kinesthetic Imagery
Impact of Thinking on Doing

Imagery to improve dance function has an illustrious lineage. Mabel Todd, a pioneer in kinesthetic anatomy, wrote an innovative book in 1937, entitled *The Thinking Body*. Her work is important to note in relation to somatic work and dance training. Lulu Sweigard worked with Todd and developed studies in ideokinetic imagery. Irene Dowd followed with her inspiring book, entitled *Taking Root to Fly*. In 1926 Todd studied body alignment and patterns of coordination. The work of Mabel Todd, linked with other somatic models, inspired a new approach to the education of dance deeply rooted in imagery. These innovative philosophies on teaching dance were integrative, linking the domain of the intellect with the realm of the body.

As founder of University of Wisconsin's dance program in 1926, Margaret H'Doubler professed the philosophy that "[dance] technique must be experienced in a way that recognizes the anatomical, physiological, and psychological connections and disciplines" (1998, p. 96). This somatic-based philosophy on dance education inspired Nancy Topf during her study with H'Doubler at Wisconsin. Nancy Topf's repatterning technique works with kinesthetic imagery as a tool for alignment, awareness, and exploration of movement vocabulary (Cho, 1998; Dixon, 2005). Currently Eric Franklin is a prolific writer of the twenty-first century, providing strategies for using imagery to dance technique. These somatic pioneers, among others, have influenced dance teachers to aid students toward improved performance and body understanding through imagery.

Recent research substantiates the premise that just thinking about something changes skeletal and muscular response in the body. A sample of the current research can be found at http://www.nytimes.com/2010/02/02/science/02angier.html?pagewanted=all&_r=0.

Thinking has a pivotal relationship to dynamic alignment and balance.

The Story: Chips the Dog with Ballon

In a modern technique class offered at Towson University's Burdick Hall, my students and I decided to try this informal experiment. The students were performing jumps at the barre. One student informally measured the height of the jump of her partner, using the lines provided by the cinderblock wall next to the barre as a reference point. Next I told the following story about Chips the dog.

On Sundays we would drive to my in-law's house outside New York City for a delicious meal of pasta with a red meat sauce. They had a miniature beagle named Chips. Each week we walked up to the front door and rang the doorbell. Chips would scurry to the door, barking. The door was solid on the bottom but had a window on the top portion. Chips jumped to try to see who it was. She would jump and jump and jump effortlessly, ears flying up, for minutes until someone unlocked the door (see Figure 3.1).

Chips had what is called ballon *in ballet technique, the appearance of lightness while jumping. The students imagined Chips and then repeated the jumps while continuing to think of the image of Chips and her head and ears flying up as they performed a few easy jumps. The students returned back to the barre and repeated the jumping exercise while the partner observed. Each student demonstrated a quantitative, measurable improvement in the height of the jumps.*

The use of imagery is a powerful teaching tool. Thinking can have a profound effect on the body to elicit or prevent improvement in dance skills. As mentioned in the first chapter, unconscious habits can also inhibit improvement. Changing your thinking can change your dancing.

Exploration: Thinking Up and Thinking Down

1. In pairs or on your own: Partner A stands in front of Partner B. Partner A closes her eyes and imagines her whole body filling with heavy wet cement from the top of the head to the feet. Take your time to sense that cement weighing down each structure of the body so the head sits heavily on the neck and the ribs sink under the weight of

FIGURE 3.1 Chips jumping. (*Source/Artist*: With permission from Hollis McCracken)

the cement onto the pelvis and the pelvis sits on the legs. Let the cement spill out your feet and fill the room so you are in cement up to your ankles . . . and then the cement hardens. Partner B gently tries to lift Partner A off the floor. If you are exploring this on your own, then try jumping a few times while maintaining the image of the cement.

2. Now Partner A imagines that her head is a hot-air balloon and the side body is like the strings and the pelvis is the basket on the balloon. At first the feet are sandbags holding it down (gravity's pull), and then imagine lift off. Partner B lifts Partner A. Again if you are experimenting with this on your own, just try a few jumps.

3. Consider these differences with your partner or consider these differences for yourself.

4. Repeat with the other person in front so each has a turn to "think up" and "think down."

Your Findings and Why They Matter

When thinking up, you are employing the deep postural support system and the body moves with more ease and efficiency. When you are thinking down, you are over-recruiting large muscle groups to engage unnecessarily and the action becomes much harder as the body ends up working its natural tendencies for poise and balance. One of the primary places to recognize unnecessary pressure down on the spine and an increased sense of weight is at the top of spine, where the first vertebra, called the atlas, meets the skull at the occiput.

The Anatomy: Clarification of the Atlanto-occipital Joint to Provide a Framework for Anatomical Imagery for "Up"

The skull has a large hole (the foramen magnum) where the spinal cord travels from the skull and the vertebrae for the spinal column for the spinal cord to disseminate nerve function through the rest of the body (see Figure 3.2). The first cervical vertebra (the atlas) articulates at the occiput to form the atlanto-occipital joint, often referred to as the AO joint (Figure 3.3). If the head is tipped back, it places pressure on the AO joint and the rest of the spine. If the face is pulled forward with eyes down, as one often does while using a cell phone, this posture also causes unnecessary stress on the spine. It is simple to discover the correct poise of this joint and to find your natural upright balance in the body. Try the following movement exploration.

Exploration: Discover Integrity of Balance at the Atlanto-occipital Joint

1. Place one finger just under the flesh behind the chin (just superior to the hyoid bone) and one at the nuchal notch at occipital ridge or base of the skull.

2. Pull the face forward to look out at this page.

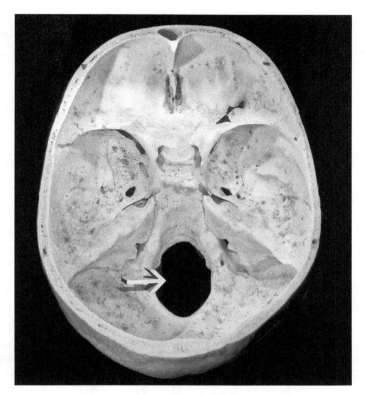

FIGURE 3.2 Foramen magnum. (*Source/author*: https://en.wikipedia.org/wiki/Foramen_magnum [public domain]; http://creativecommons.org/licenses/by-sa/3.0/)

3. Notice what happens at the base of the skull. Pull the chin and neck back into "straight posture" that we as dancers often think is needed to align the spine. Sense the front of the neck and jaw. The skull is actually pressing down on the spine in both of these movements, so the head feels heavy and there is more tension in the muscles of the neck.

4. Explore a balance between the head and neck where the head feels easeful and poised to balance. This balance requires less effort and feels more relaxed.

The above exercise was inspired by the work of Judy Leibowitz while she was teaching at The Juilliard School (see Further Readings).

Your Findings and Why They Matter

Once the AO joint is balanced, the deep muscles of the spine can support the body with ease. Chips the dog displayed this beautiful dynamic alignment each week as she jumped at the front door. For dancers these deep muscles and the poise of the head provide strong integrity for the complicated actions needed to jump, turn, or balance on one leg. If the AO joint is compressed, the rest of the body responds with tension.

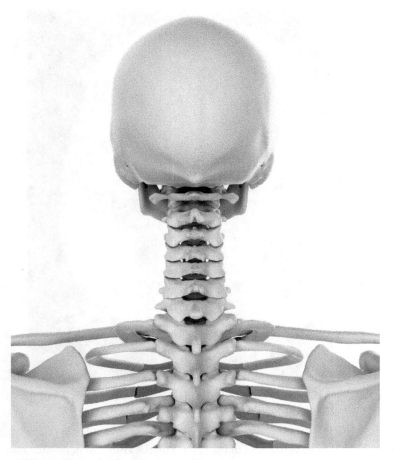

FIGURE 3.3 AO joint. (*Source/author*: Shutterstock)

Mindfulness in Dance Class

Notice if your chin likes to lift up as you prepare for a turn or jump. See if you can reassess this, release unnecessary tension, and balance the AO joint to allow for efficient muscle recruitment. If you spend most of your day with your AO joint in imbalance, it is difficult to discover this balance easily when you are preparing to balance or turn.

Think about Chips' ears flying up as you practice jumps during class. Or just think "up" so the head leads the movement into the air rather than pushing up from your feet.

Mindfulness in Daily Life

When walking from a car or train into work, or from your dorm to class, take a moment to "think down" and see how that affects how your body feels. No need to judge the sensation, just notice. Now "think up" and see what happens.

4

Deep Muscles of Postural Support

When we are infants and toddlers, we naturally balance the head and sit and stand with a lengthened spine. As we get older unconscious habits interfere with this natural balance. One does not have to grip to stand up or work hard to sit up straight. The body has an inherent system of balance.

For people to regain this natural poise, it helps to first think or imagine the skeletal structure in order for the muscular system to act efficiently. If the skeletal structure is balanced through the center of gravity (COG), the postural muscles will activate. The pull-down from gravity elicits the response for the muscles to suspend the skeletal system upright with ease. If the head is pulled forward off the COG or there is an imbalance at the feet, the body exhibits a lack of efficiency in motion and muscular overuse occurs.

The Story: Discovering Gravity's Effect on Posture

In the 1960s, NASA scientists were focused on the space race to the moon. During the Apollo missions with three astronauts in the capsule, the astronauts were in a weightless environment for longer and longer periods of time. The astronauts would "splash down" to Earth by landing in the ocean. The astronauts were carried out in huge cargo nets onto the ship. Once on board, it became apparent that they could not stand! It took up to a week for some of them to regain standing balance. This led the support team to think there was muscle atrophy in space, so they designed ways for the astronauts to maintain large group muscle function through resistance training. The astronauts prepared for the next mission, flew into space and returned, but still could not stand up for days after the return from the weightless environment in the space capsule. The team realized that a group of postural support muscles very close along the spine are autonomic. These muscles lengthen the spine and support the body in upright posture every day as a natural "righting system" for balanced movement. They contain slow twitch or Type 1 muscle fibers, rich in mitochondria, which enable them to function constantly and effortlessly for long periods of time, but they require a trigger. This trigger is gravity. When gravity pulls down, these muscles then engage to lengthen and support the body in upright posture. Standing and dancing is the delicate relationship with gravity and energy. Hence, gravity is not a force weighing us down; it is the impulse for us to stand up!

The Anatomy: Type 1 Muscles of Postural Support

The deep postural muscles help us interact with gravity in a resilient fashion. If we interfere with these deep stabilizing muscles, the much larger muscles of the back begin to execute the muscular effort required. One can perform the task of upright posture with the larger, more superficial muscles, but this requires more effort, uses much more energy, and the muscles become fatigued more quickly. The body experiences this fatigue as tension or pain.

The muscles illustrated in Figure 4.1 are known collectively as the suboccipital muscles. These muscles are predominantly local stabilizers. If the skeletal system is in balance, they can work autonomically and tirelessly to maintain balance of the head and neck.

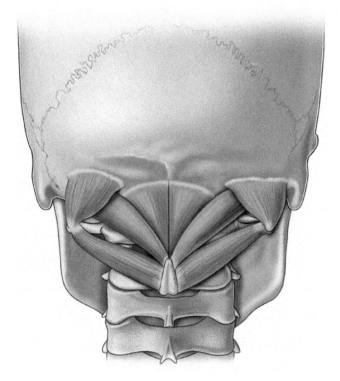

FIGURE 4.1 Suboccipital muscles. (Functional Awareness® and artist Caitlin Duckwall)

Figure 4.1 illustrates the four specific muscles of the suboccipitals: the rectus capitis posterior major and minor and the obliquus capitis superior and inferior. They are short muscles with limited mobility. They aid in extension, side bending of the cervical spine, and limited rotation at C1 and C2 (nodding yes and no). These muscles function constantly and subconsciously to maintain spinal balance while we are sitting, standing, walking, and dancing. They are primarily what are called Type 1 or stabilizing muscle fibers.

In addition to the suboccipital muscles, another primary Type 1 muscle group for postural support is the transversospinalis. The transversospinalis group is comprised of three sets of muscles that are very deep along the spine and run superomedially from transverse process to spinous process. The rotatores span one vertebra and are closest to the spine. The multifidus muscles span three vertebral levels and lie just superficial to the rotatores. The semispinalis is the most superficial muscle and spans five or six vertebral levels. These muscles aid extension, flexion, and rotation, depending on their responses to other muscles, but they are pivotally important for upright posture. Together they form a strong "braid" or chevron along the spine to allow for spinal mobility and postural stability (Figure 4.2).

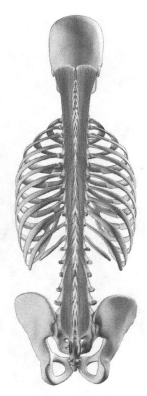

FIGURE 4.2 Transversospinalis muscle group. (*Source/author*: Functional Awareness® and artist Caitlin Duckwall)

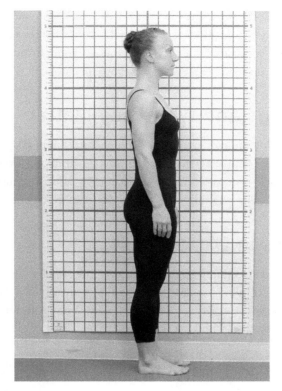

FIGURE 4.3 Points of balance. (*Source/author*: With permission from Jim Burger Photography)

Understanding the inherent muscle structure to support a lengthening spine is useful to discovering efficiency of movement and freedom from unnecessary effort and tension. As dancers, we often think that demonstrating effort and tension is a good thing, but unnecessary effort impedes expressivity.

If the body is balanced through the COG (Figure 4.3), the Type 1 muscles of the transversospinalis fire easily, tirelessly, and without pain. The pull downward from gravity elicits the response for the muscles to suspend the skeletal system upright with ease. You were experiencing this ease of motion in the first movement exploration in Chapter 3, called "thinking up and thinking down." Gravity, pulling us to the earth, provides a trigger for these muscles to activate and sustain us in dynamic alignment.

Exploration: Kinesthetic Sensing of the Transversospinalis Muscles

Put your arms at your side and hands resting with the third finger facing your leg at the side seams of your pants. Take a moment to envision the poise of the head, the balance at the tripod of your feet, and the plumb line of balance through the ears, shoulders, hips, and ankles.

Stretch and extend your fingers toward the ground to enhance the pull of gravity and then "think up" to engage the transversospinalis. You will often feel a sensation of the spine lengthening energetically. If you have a partner, let your partner tug at the fingers to enhance this sensation. If you are on your own, you can use small free weights.

Your Findings and Why They Matter

When thinking up, you are employing the deep postural support system and the body moves with more ease and efficiency. When you are thinking down, you are over-recruiting large muscle groups to engage unnecessarily and the action becomes much harder as the body ends up working its natural tendencies for balance.

Mindfulness in Dance Class

Many exercises in dance training begin with a musical preparation. During these moments of preparation, think of pressing the tripod on your feet into the floor and "think up" through your whole spine. Do not "pull" for up. The body and transversospinalis will engage to naturally lengthen with your thinking.

Mindfulness in Daily Life

When carrying grocery bags from the store, distribute the weight of the bags evenly between your two hands. As practiced in the movement exploration above, "think up" as the weight of the bags pull down. This counterbalance between gravity and energy improves dynamic alignment and whole health for your back.

5

Motions of the Trunk and Elegant Use of Spiral

The balance of upright posture is an excellent place to begin the discoveries in ease of movement, but the body moves in a myriad of wonderful ways to satisfy a required skill or activity. Dancers train to be adaptable to many movements with varied tempos and phrasing. It is possible to enrich this training through skeletal and muscular awareness. Sensing a connection from the head through the pelvis to the feet facilitates a primary organization to allow spirals, twists, and innovative creative movements to unfold. There are tremendous benefits in exploring somatics-based dance training and embodied anatomy to enhance movement potential in the spiral motions of the spine.

The Story: Dancing for a Lifetime

It was a warm summer evening in New England. We were in a black box theater at Dean College in Franklin, Massachusetts. At seventy-five years old, master dancer, choreographer, educator, and performer Bill Evans performed not just one but two solo works on the program. When onstage, his body exudes a litheness that belies his years. He moves through the space with a connectivity and expressivity that draws you in to the smallest gesture and surprises you when the movement darts through space (see Figure 5.1).

He embodies the resiliency and elasticity inherent in the spiral nature of our neuromuscular system and transforms the movement from "steps" into art. He has been performing since he was nine. During much of his career, he has been in a deep practice of embodied anatomy and somatics-based dancing. His practice inhibits limitation and permits possibility.

The body is not composed of straight lines and right angles. It is an elegant design of curves and spirals to provide resilient strength. The resilient nature of the spine and the supporting muscular and myofascial system is a wonderful spiral web to provide choices in movement. Dance master Bill Evans embodies the inherent design of the possible

FIGURE 5.1 William (Bill) Evans. Photo credit: Jim Dusen

movements in the trunk. Exploring movement activities along with anatomical information enhances the awareness of body functioning, and the body can release habitual holding to develop increased flexibility and strength. The following exploration reveals information about one's individual spinal flexibility.

Exploration: Discovery of Spinal Preferences

A. Spinal Roll Down from the Wall: Flexion and Extension
   1. Lean with your back against the wall and your heels 4 inches away from the wall. Place your feet a comfortable distance apart and in parallel, and begin to roll down. Instead of rolling down by moving away from the wall, try pressing each vertebra or part of the spine into the wall and then roll down bringing your head toward the floor. The effect feels like the inside of a wave as it crests. This movement allows the body to sense the spine and where it articulates easily with the wall and where it moves in chunks away from the wall.

2. Gently bend the knees and keep them slightly bent as you roll back up the wall, seeing if you can feel the vertebrae connecting back to the wall.
3. Repeat Steps 1 and 2 one more time.
4. See if you notice any difference in your overall contact with the wall and in your dynamic elasticity of the back.
5. Now step away from the wall completely. Perform a spinal roll down without the wall for support. See if this spinal articulation is now different from your habitual manner of rolling forward.

B. Side Bending Right and Left: Lateral Flexion
1. Once again along the wall, with the legs in a wide second position and arms overhead in a wide V, how far can you bend to the side? Can you bend the same amount to the other side?
2. Does the sensation of stretch on the side of your body feel equal on both sides?

C. Spiraling to the Right and Left: Spinal Rotation Right and Rotation Left
1. Step away from the wall and place your feet in a wide parallel position. Consider the tripod of balance at the feet and the balance of the head.
2. Close your eyes and turn your head and spine to the right, letting the arms wrap around your torso.
3. Open your eyes and see how far you have turned.
4. Now repeat to the other side. Is it easier to turn your head and spine one direction than the other?

Your Findings and Why They Matter

Daily habits can affect our ability to twist, turn, and maintain flexibility for dance performance. Habit can create stiffness and lack of mobility in specific areas of the spine and torso over time. For example, if you always sleep with your head turned to one side, these many hours in one position create a flexibility to turn to that side and develop a restriction of movement on the other side over time. If you always tuck one knee up tight to your chest when sleeping, this position creates an imbalance in the pelvis and sacroiliac joint and muscular imbalances in the back and also the deep psoas muscle of anterior postural and pelvic support. The imbalanced rotation for long periods of time during sleep has an affect on the ability to turn more efficiently in one direction more than the other direction. Understanding the anatomy is a key to understanding body patterns.

The Anatomy: Spinal Curves

The spine has several sections and each one has a slight curve that provides a resiliency in the structure for adaptive movement. The cervical, thoracic, lumbar, and sacral sections contain curves that support the range of movement of the torso. The seven bones of the neck are called cervical vertebrae, as discussed in Chapter 1. The twelve thoracic verte-brae each have costal bones or ribs that are attached to their transverse processes. The five lumbar vertebrae connect the ribs to the pelvis, and the five fused bones of the sacrum create the end of the spine with the one to three fused bones of the coccyx comprising the inferior tip. When viewed from the side the spinal column has four curves. The cervi-cal spine curves slightly inward. The thoracic spine curves slightly outward. In the lower portion, the lumbar spine curves inward with the sacrum slightly outward. The curves provide a range of motion between flexion and extension in the torso. People can display some imbalances in the spinal curvature as illustrated in Figure 5.2.

Lordosis (swayback) is the shape of the spine in the lower back. Doctors use the term hyperlordosis for curves that are greater than usual. The term kyphosis is used to describe the thoracic spinal curve that results in a hunched or rounded back. Scoliosis is an abnormal lateral curvature of the spine. In scoliosis the spine curves to the side, and each vertebra also rotates on the next one in a corkscrew fashion.

If one section of the spine has excessive curvature, the balance of resiliency is upset and the body develops patterns of overuse and tension. In some cases these curves are a genetic feature and passed down through families. This condition is called idiopathic

(a)

FIGURE 5.2 (A) Lordosis, (B) kyphosis, and (C) scoliosis. (*Source/author*: With permission from Jim Burger Photography)

(b)

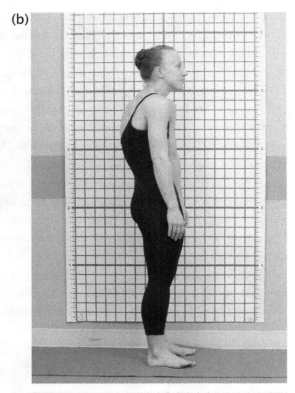

(c)

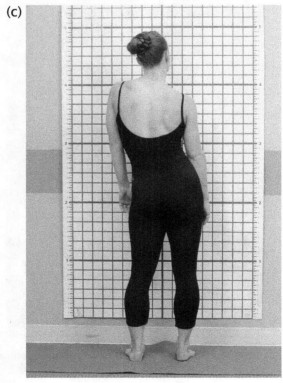

FIGURE 5.2 Continued

scoliosis or idiopathic kyphosis. These conditions require medical guidance and at times might require surgery; however, these conditions can be mitigated with exercises, braces, and mindfulness to daily habits. Most of the time these curves develop as a result of postural habits and overuse. This condition is called postural scoliosis or postural kyphosis. These conditions can be changed through attention to daily movement habits and reconditioning the muscles of the trunk to support a balance in the spinal curves.

The spine can move in four basic ways: flexion, extension, lateral bending, and lateral rotation. Dance forms combine these movements in a myriad of creative ways to elicit nonverbal expression. Developing a nonjudgmental awareness of where your spine moves easily and where it resists movement can open up the possibility to change this pattern to allow for greater ease and potential for movement.

Mindfulness in Dance Class

Just before class starts, practice roll down from the wall, side bending at the wall, and the rotation sequence from the movement exploration above to discover the flexibility of the spine. Or after class let your spine discover neutral from the rigors of class by rolling down from the wall.

Between exercises in class, consider the tripod of the feet and balance of the head, aligning the curves of the spine, and recovering from the joys and demands of twists, turns, side bending, and contractions required in class. It is a moment to pause and press reset for your body.

Mindfulness in Daily Life

Getting out of a car or spiraling out of a chair each day after a meal is a delightful place to engage in the elegant use of the spiral musculature for ease in action. Let your eyes and head lead the turn and let the whole spine follow. Let the body freely move around the spine and press the feet into the floor to help propel you out of the chair.

It is not about getting it right, it is about the opportunity to bring your attention to spiral movements during daily tasks, making the mundane playful and fun. This movement can improve your expressivity in dance class, particularly for work with cambre, upper, middle, and low back curves, contractions, and X roll variations, as well as all the other spiral movements in the body.

The Pelvis as Conduit
from Head to Feet

One of the most common concerns for dancers is alignment of the pelvis. Dance students frequently complain of hip pain, low back pain, and knee pain. This is often related to mal-coordinated, unconscious movement patterns of the hips in relation to the head, spine, and legs. Inaccurate understanding of pelvic engagement can impede dynamic alignment and inhibit lateral rotation, or turnout. Learning skeletal and muscular landmarks and their relationship to movement patterning can often create a shift in habitual use of the pelvis for more efficient action. Visualizing the anatomical landmarks accurately allows dancers to acknowledge habit and reassess their movement to better support the pelvic structure through the rigors of dance training.

The Story: Ballet Dancer Duck Walk

A talented dancer and dance educator who performed with American Ballet Theater and on the Broadway stage, started to experience chronic pain in her hips while walking and limitations in turnout during passé, retiré, and développé. We noticed two interesting habits in her that were having a significant impact on daily activity and dancing. During her everyday actions and in dance class, her toes were always pointing out to the sides as if she was standing rotated in first or second position. Standing turned out was the norm for her hips and legs, not just the practice during class. Ballet is a beautiful art form that requires rigorous hours of practice, but continuing to turn out all day, every day, actually impedes the resilient balance of the myofascial and neuromuscular system surrounding the hip from performing efficiently, limits range of motion, and can cause pain.

Exploration: Common Mismapping of the Hip Socket

1. Point to where you think your femur, or thigh bone, meets the pelvis at the hip socket.
2. Make a note of this spot. When asked to point to the hip socket, many people are uncertain where this joint is located. They will point to their greater trochanter, located on the thigh or femur bone, or often people point at their waist at the top of the iliac crest.
3. Place your hand on what is commonly known as the hip bone or the iliac crest at the anterior superior iliac spine (ASIS) and begin to move your hand toward the pubic bone. You will feel a softer space or indent. This area is the anterior portion of the ball-and-socket joint of the hip, where the head of the femur rests in the socket called the acetabulum (see Figure 6.1).
4. Leave your fingers here and march in place. You will notice this area folding. This motion is the head of the femur gliding in the socket to allow for hip flexion, and the muscles that primarily flex the hip are located on this anterior side. For many the location of the hip socket is a surprising revelation.

Your Findings and Why They Matter

When one unconsciously has a faulty body map of where a joint action occurs, the brain recruits muscle action based on this inaccurate information and the body then moves

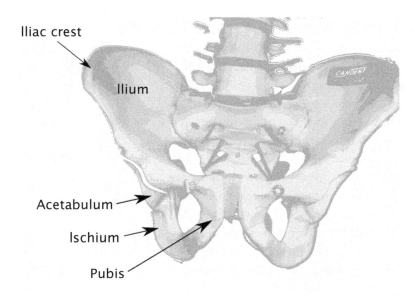

FIGURE 6.1 Skeletal landmarks of the hip. (*Source/author*: https://commons.wikimedia.org/wiki/File:Pelvis_diagram.png [public domain])

inefficiently. Often the lateral or outside muscles of the leg and hip are more developed than the more medial muscles. This unconscious mismapping of the hip in relation to the leg can create a muscular and myofascial imbalance and contribute to snapping hip syndrome, low back pain, a tight iliotibial band, or patella tendinitis (jumper's knee). Fortunately, the brain and body are very adaptable. It is easy to rethink and discover a body map with greater structural integrity. Functional awareness of hip rotation and pelvic alignment are key to improving dance technique and maintaining whole body health over time.

The Anatomy: Skeletal and Muscular Considerations for Pelvic Alignment

The hip joint, or acetabular femoral joint, is a complex structure. It is the conduit from the torso to the legs. It is a ball-and-socket joint. The rounded head of the femur bone fits into the concave structure of the acetabulum of the pelvis. A ball-and-socket joint facilitates flexion, extension, adduction, abduction, medial rotation, and lateral rotation.

Figure 6.1 shows that the acetabulum (hip socket) is midway between the highest ridge of the pelvic bone (ASIS) and the pubis. This location is where you were feeling the indent when you were marching in place during the movement exploration above.

The hip joint has a complex muscular support system. A few key muscles are useful to know for improving dance training and daily balance. One key support muscle for hip flexion that links the torso to the legs is the psoas major, as seen in Figure 6.2. It is the muscle closest to the spine in the front or anterior side and attaches to the bodies of the vertebrae of the spine. The psoas is the deepest muscle anteriorly and is similar to the transversospinalis muscle because it contains stabilizing Type 1 muscle fibers to support the body in upright posture. This muscle interdigitates with the iliacus to form a common tendon called the iliopsoas tendon. The psoas major also contains Type 2 or mobilizing fibers to support movements of dynamic action. It is a strong flexor of the hip and the only muscle that flexes the hip beyond 90 degrees. It is a primary muscle of effective développé as is discussed later in the chapter.

The pelvis has a wide range of movement. It can move through all the positions for jazz isolations. It can sustain an undercurve for a modern dance contraction. The beautiful art form of dance explores the end ranges of movement for the pelvis depending on the aesthetic. The important concept to understand through Functional Awareness® is that the body will be in pain if you maintain these end ranges for too long or carry them into your daily life habits.

Pelvic neutral is not a position. Rather it is a range in which the body can sustain upright balance and sitting with the least amount of stress (Figure 6.3c). Anterior tilt is when the pelvis tips and often exhibits a sway in the low back (lordosis) (Figure 6.3a). Posterior tilt is when the pelvis is tucked under as in a contraction in the low back and looks more like a letter C (Figure 6.3b). Try each pelvic position for yourself and exaggerate the sensation. You will begin to feel where the stress is revealed.

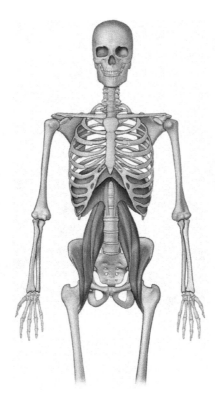

FIGURE 6.2 The psoas and diaphragm. (*Source/author*: Functional Awareness® and artist Caitlin Duckwall)

Figure 6.3D displays a dancer in forward sway. This position is when the pelvis may be in neutral or tucked under (posterior tilt) and, in addition, the center of gravity has been moved forward toward the balls of the feet too far, upsetting the plumb line of balance in the whole system. In dance this is a common way for dancers to move over the balls of the feet for relevé. Unfortunately, this stance places stress on the low back, knees, and hips. Moving the whole body structure toward equal weight at the tripod of the feet is a more efficient model for dynamic alignment than pushing the pelvis forward. Figure 6.3D demonstrates forward sway while in neutral pelvis. The ABT dancer in the story at the beginning of this chapter was holding on to forward sway all day. This placed undue strain on her hip joint and caused unnecessary wear and discomfort over time.

Try the following movement exploration to discover more about your personal habits in pelvic balance.

Exploration: Anterior Tip, Posterior Tip, and Forward Sway

Begin by practicing some of the anatomical imagery presented in the previous chapters. Consider the tripod of balance at the feet. Allow yourself to imagine the balance of the

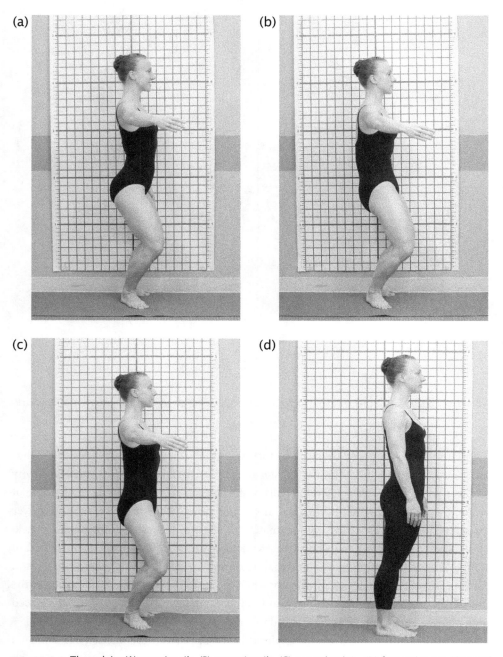

FIGURE 6.3 The pelvis: (A) anterior tilt, (B) posterior tilt, (C) neutral pelvis, (D) forward sway. (*Source/author*: With permission from Jim Burger Photography)

head on the spine and the AO joint. Remember, if you balance at the feet and consider the poise of the head, many unnecessary muscle actions release in order for you to recruit into dynamic alignment with efficiency.

This exercise can be explored on your own or with a partner. If you are working with a partner, ask permission to place your hands on the partner.

1. Partner A stands in parallel position of the feet.
2. Partner B's hands are placed onto the skeletal structures of the pelvis: one hand on the ASIS and one hand gently on the sacrum. The sacrum is the triangular-shaped bone at the base of the spinal vertebrae.
3. Have Partner A bend the knees and straighten them in a plié motion. Partner B, notice if the pelvis tips forward or back in your hands.
4. Partner A goes up on his or her toes in a relevé motion and Partner B senses and observes the change in pelvic position, if any.
5. Partner A considers a neutral place for the pelvis. Partner B, observe if Partner A can maintain that while going through plié and relevé again.

Your Findings and Why They Matter

Pelvic neutral is a place to maintain or move through, not a position to grip. The pelvis and spine do have a slight movement when moving through plié and relevé. If you grip or preserve the position of the pelvis with too much tension, it can place unnecessary strain on the ligaments and tendons, resulting in pain at the front of the hips or in the lower back.

The pelvis is not an isolated structure. Consider the tripod of balance at your feet and the poise of the head before shifting pelvic alignment. Releasing the initial habit, then recruiting necessary muscular support to sustain a dynamic pelvic alignment, creates greater efficiency and less stress.

The Anatomy: Muscular Considerations for Turnout

Lateral rotation (turnout) is a specific aesthetic and requirement in many contemporary and classical dance forms. This movement initiates at the hip socket. The biggest muscular misconception for dancers is that practicing turnout all day improves their turnout. They often consciously or unconsciously walk in turnout, stand in turnout, and sleep turned out. This constant activation of one set of muscle fibers without opportunity for recoil and recuperation places increased stress on the ligaments supporting the hip. In short, standing and walking turned out all the time does not improve turnout. It impedes elasticity and resiliency of joint motion. This is the secondary factor in the ABT dancer's hip restrictions and pain. One of the primary groups of muscles used to recruit turnout

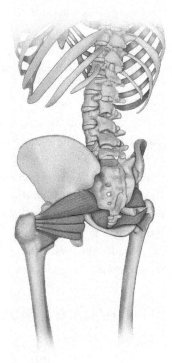

FIGURE 6.4 Deep lateral rotators of the hip. (*Source/author*: Functional Awareness® and artist Caitlin Duckwall)

in the hip are called the deep lateral rotators. The six deep lateral rotators of the hip are the quadratus femoris, obturator externus, obturator internus, superior gemellus, inferior gemellus, and piriformis (see Figure 6.4).

Exploration: Recruiting the Deep Lateral Rotators

1. Repeat previous exploration above, but change the foot position to first or second position turned out.
2. If you have a Balanced Body Rotator Disc, repeat both explorations for neutral pelvis in parallel, first, and second on the discs. The Rotator Disc is very effective for discovering the necessary muscular recruitment needed to sustain turnout.
3. If you do not have a Rotator Disc, wearing a pair of nylon socks can also supply the glide needed to practice the activity in Step 2. Cotton socks are less effective for this exploration. Cotton often has more friction with the floor and not enough slide to permit the femur to rotate in the acetabulum easily.

Exploration: Myofascial Release of Deep Lateral Rotators

1. Find a small ball that you can use for self-massage. The ball can range in hardness from a lacrosse or tennis ball, to a softer ball such as a Nerf ball. Take some time to discover the ideal ball and pressure that works for you.
2. Lie down in semi-supine position, on your back with both knees bent.
3. Place one ball under the right buttocks. Allow for several gentle cycles of breathing in your own timing. Allow the muscle tissue to release around the ball. Let go of tension in this experience.
4. Slide the right leg out gently to straighten the knee with the ball still in place. Pause, allow for a breath, and then return. Do this twice.
5. Let both knees drop to the right while the ball is still in place and take a moment to breathe here in this position.
6. Return to semi-supine and remove the ball. Slide the right leg out to straighten the knee and then the left. Notice if there is a difference between the two legs.
7. Repeat on the other side.

Your Findings and Why They Matter

After performing the exercise on the right leg, did you notice a difference between the right and the left leg? Many people feel the right leg is longer or more relaxed than the left. The sensation often equalizes after performing the exercise on both legs. This exploration releases neuromuscular myofascial tissue to release unnecessary tension and provide resilience in action.

Mindfulness in Dance Class

As you practice a dance phrase during class, be consciously aware of the various movements needed in the pelvis. Experiment with pelvic neutral during a phrase that travels across the floor. Investigate the various other pelvic tilts that are possible (anterior tilt, posterior tilt, forward sway). Different dance forms employ many possible pelvic orientations depending on that style of movement. Observe the choreographer's intention and bring a clarity regarding the pelvis to your dancing. At the end of the exploration in the dance phrase, return to pelvic neutral as well as an awareness of the tripod of the feet and the balance of the head to allow for recuperation and restoration.

Mindfulness in Daily Life

If you practice dynamic alignment in dance class but ignore it the rest of the day, it compromises the progress your body can make toward improving range of motion and technical skills in dance training. While brushing your teeth or doing dishes, notice your feet and gently move them toward neutral.

In addition notice your habitual stance for pelvic tilt. Without judgment, assess this pelvic tilt and gently shift your body toward a balanced neutral. As a tool for discovering neutral pelvis, return to your tripod of the feet and balance at the AO joint. Notice if your pelvis finds its way back to neutral without having to create the position. If it needs more encouragement, picture the bony landmarks of your pelvis and allow for ease in action. Asking yourself to make this pelvic shift in daily use will deepen your motor sensory map for pelvic neutral, and improve your ability to access this pelvic support during dance practice and performance.

Ways of Walking
How Gait Affects Dance Training

Walking is propelling the body's center of gravity, or plumb line of standing, forward in space. Walking is an effective recuperation tool and whole health activity. We learn to walk when we are very young, yet we are never taught how to do so biomechanically. Movement patterns that form, as early as crawling, affect our skeletal structure, muscle structure, and myofascial tissue. Walking, like standing, can promote balance, or it can systemically compromise the spine and become a source of discomfort. Habit plays an important role in the choices one makes for walking. Functional Awareness® works with people to retrain walking patterns to enable greater efficiency and stability.

The Story: Allegra and the Cobbler

I live in Brooklyn, New York. In the city it is common for people to take more than 10,000 steps per day! With that much walking, anyone would need to send his or her shoes to a cobbler. This is why there are shoe repair places all over New York City. I have a pair of boots that I love. I continually need the soles replaced, so I can continue to wear them even after I've worn out the soles. On my third trip to replace the heels of my boots, Victor, the cobbler, pointed out that I am constantly wearing out one spot on my left heel more than the rest. Aha! This was an amazing observation, since I regularly have left ankle pain and discomfort. My shoes were a clue to what my habit was in walking and the reason for my discomfort in my ankle. I strike heavily on the outside of my left heel more than my right and not evenly through my foot. Thanks to Victor, I had a better understanding of what my habit was in walking.

The act of walking is a combination of our structure, our understanding of function, and our habitual body actions. One delight in being human is our systems are very adaptable to change. Knowing a bit about how "the suit fits," allows us to reconsider how walking affects dancing. Take a look at the bottom of your favorite shoes. Where are they worn out? Does this reflect where you keep your weight in walking and standing?

The first thing we look at when working with injured dancers is walking. As discussed in Chapter 6, using the turnout muscles or deep lateral rotators of the hip constantly in everyday life impedes natural hip function, places undo stress on the lower back and sacroiliac joint, and creates wear at the iliofemoral ligament. Walking with the toes pointed out is a common habit for many people. This constant recruitment of the deep lateral rotators can create less resilience in the hip structure. It does not improve dance skills. It just feels comfortable, as it is how your "suit fits." In repatterning walking you can regain bilateral range of rotation as well as improve stability on the standing leg.

Exploration: Stepping into Someone Else's Shoes

This activity can be done in partners or without a partner by recording yourself and watching the video.

1. Partner A begins by standing in a comfortable stance. Partner B first observes this body stance from a side view and then from the back or posterior view.
2. Partner A begins to walk around the room and Partner B follows, imitating or mirroring the walk of the person in front.
3. Partner A begins to notice asymmetry or idiosyncrasies about his or her own walk. Partner A starts to exaggerate these so they become evident to Partner B, who is following behind. Partner B takes on these new exaggerations.
4. Partner A increases the exaggeration a little more with Partner B following behind.
5. Finally Partner A steps away while Partner B continues to walk, in order for Partner A to see his or her exaggerated habit. Discuss your findings.

Your Findings and Why They Matter

As noted in standing, small unconscious habits create subtle imbalances in walking as well. We do not feel them as pain often during the day, but the repercussions from these habits affect the system. If you walk for 5 minutes in an exaggerated manner of your habit, you reveal the muscle stress that would occur in regular walking over the course of a day. This movement exploration demonstrates the muscular impact your habits have on the body.

The Anatomy: An Introduction to Biomechanical Considerations in Gait

Gait, or walking, is as complex as a leap or turn in dancing. Each person has a unique walk, and in coaching gait efficiency, there is not one set of tips to address everyone's issues. It is useful to become functionally aware of a few key points within gait to elicit greater ease and balance. This mindfulness will aid the body in recuperation from activity instead of contributing imbalanced action to fatigue the body further.

Walking involves movement through the whole body. We will take a closer look specifically at the motions required of the hip, knee, and ankle. The ankle (talocrural joint), a synovial hinge joint, has the potential for flexion and extension. Other movements such as rolling out (inversion) or rolling in (eversion), are actually movements that occur in the other thirty joints of the foot. The knee, as a hinge joint, mostly moves through flexion and extension (though it does have about 3 to 5 degrees of rotation on average available for resiliency). The hip, as a ball-and-socket joint, has a large range of motion and has the potential for many different actions: flexion, extension, abduction, adduction, and medial and lateral rotation. Walking is a movement predominantly forward in the sagittal plane; thus all three joints in the leg have to move through flexion and extension to create the gait cycle.

The gait cycle begins when one foot strikes the ground in front of you and it ends when the same foot strikes the ground again. There are two phases in gait: the stance phase and the swing phase (Figure 7.1).

Stance Phase

Stance phase occurs when a foot is in contact with the earth. This phase includes the initial heel strike of the foot in dorsiflexion on the ground, a rolling through the weight of the foot, and then propulsion off the ball of the foot in plantarflexion to propel the leg to begin to swing forward.

Swing Phase

Swing phase is when the foot is not in contact with the earth and the leg is literally swinging from extension to flexion. Once the foot propels off in the back, the leg swings freely to travel forward.

This seemingly simple motion truly involves the whole body from heels to head. Flexion and extension occur at the ankle, the knee, and the hip. Rotation occurs as a

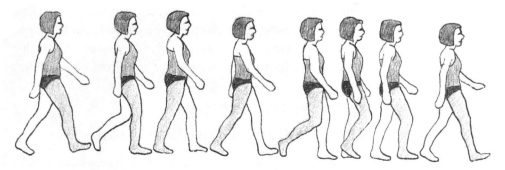

FIGURE 7.1 Phases of the gait cycle. (*Source/artist*: Hollis McCracken)

ripple effect up the spine and flexion and extension reverberate into the shoulder joint to create the swinging of our arms. There are many places throughout our bodies in which we can slightly alter our gait to create grinding, pulling, twisting, straining, or misalignment in the body. The moment the leg moves into slight medial or lateral rotation and does not track correctly, strain is put on the entire leg structure and can create pain over time. Recall the habits you noted in standing; how would these very same habits affect your walking? As we mature, we develop idiosyncrasies in our walking habits. As seen in the cobbler story, these idiosyncrasies are sometimes evident by looking at the bottom of the shoes you wear most frequently while walking. You discovered some of these in the walking exploration. These habits can facilitate ease of motion or they can compromise the system. The following exploration is one approach to discovering easeful walking through Functional Awareness®, to allow for a release from habit, and an opportunity to choose new patterns stepping forward.

Exploration: Biomechanical Ease in Walking

1. Start to walk. Notice what part of your body leads out first. Many of us lead with our face or push forward with the pelvis. Some people flick a straight leg out first. What do you notice? Keep this in mind to notice if this is happening today or if it is a frequent habit.

(a)

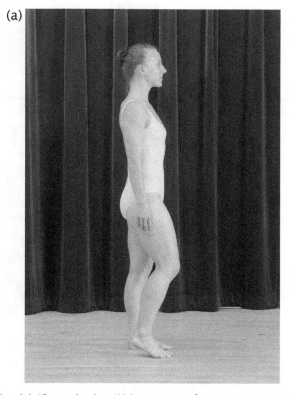

FIGURE 7.2 Peel and pedal. (*Source/author*: With permission from Jim Burger Photography)

(b)

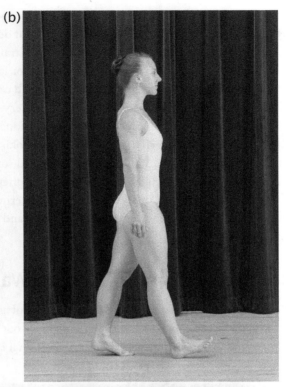

(c)

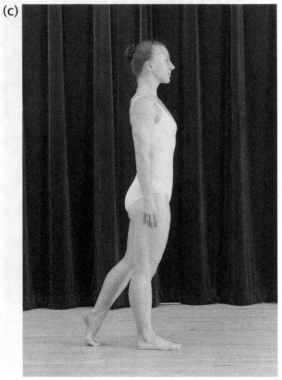

FIGURE 7.2 Continued

(d)

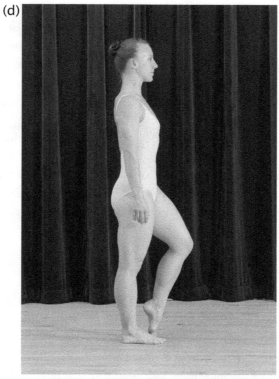

(e)

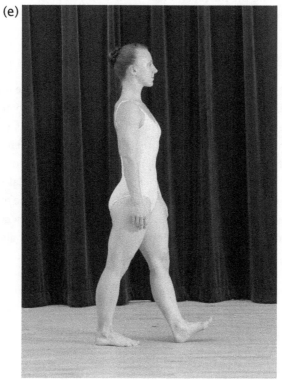

FIGURE 7.2 Continued

2. Stand once again with equal weight on both legs. Consider the tripod of balance at the feet and gaze out at eye level to visualize the AO joint and poise of the head. Think up, not down.

3. Recruit for efficient motor control. Slightly shift your weight to the right leg as you peel your left foot off the floor and propel or push off the ball of the left foot (see Figure 7.2). This is called *peel and pedal.* Continue to peel and pedal from one leg to the other.

4. When walking, the knee should be the first body part to break the plane forward, not the face and head or the pelvis.

5. The most common issue for people who experience pain from walking and running is their over stride, taking steps that swing too far from the body's center of gravity. Try smaller steps at a quicker tempo when you are in a hurry instead of large steps that overexert the system.

Mindfulness in Dance Class

Large strides with turned-out legs during leaps and runs are beautiful and part of the aesthetics in some forms of dance. Recover from that required action in everyday life by letting the feet be more toward parallel and the stride to balance within an easeful leg swing.

During a traveling phrase across the floor, notice what part of the body leads. Does your habit for initiating the movement lead first? Can you pause, allow for a breath, and rethink the movement initiation required for that phase?

Mindfulness in Daily Life

As you walk from your car into work or into the dance class, take a moment to "think up" instead of down to lengthen the back of your body from heel to head. Next allow the many joints of the lower limb to bring you to your destination as you peel and pedal. Notice the rhythm of your foot strike. Is the rhythm even from left to right or do you favor one side more than the other? Think about this rhythm in your body and see if it allows the body to become more symmetrical pedal-a-pedal-a-pedal-a-pedal-a.

Check your own shoes to see if they wear out more on one shoe more than the other. Does it wear more on one portion of the foot? How does this observation relate to the movement explorations performed earlier? What can you discover about how you move through life?

Breath as the Deep Central Support for Dancing

One of the fundamental systems of the body is the respiratory system. We breathe automatically and unconsciously. We also can use the breathing mechanism in intricate ways with conscious control. For example, singers, horn players, and actors control breath to achieve amazing artistic results. The breathing mechanism supports neuromuscular stamina and cardiovascular health. Breathing is not always a fundamental aspect of many forms of dance training, yet it is at the heart of creating expressivity and phrasing in all forms of dance.

Breath is both autonomic and muscularly controlled. As we have musculoskeletal habits, we also have unconscious habits for breathing. Exploring a few functional principles for respiratory action in relation to breathing habit provides possibilities to improve respiratory function, reduce excess tension and stress, and improve expressivity in movement.

The Story: Breath Support in Performance

We were attending a choral concert of young talented middle school singers from the entire county in Maryland. The auditorium was packed with parents and friends of these aspiring vocal artists on a warm Sunday in May. As they began the second piece on the program, one of the singers suddenly fainted, but safely came to sit on the bleachers. The singer was helped by a parent, and the conductor moved along through the piece. We could see the anxiety in the students rise along with their adrenaline from being onstage, and they began to then tighten in their backs and knees and tense in their vocal system. As the program progressed, another student fainted, and then another, and another. It resembled the hysteria of the Salem witch trials with young women dropping left and right until there were parents onstage along the sides of the bleachers to help students who fainted to recover safely. All the while the choral director was attempting to let the show go on. At intermission the *students were in a panic about returning to the stage again for fear they might faint. Under the anxiety and stress, students began to tighten the low back and knees. This action inhibits the diaphragmatic movement needed for singing. In turn the students were taking air in predominantly through the mouth, leading to CO_2 accumulation in the lungs and a condition often referred to as shallow water blackout, which caused them to faint. A little functional awareness could have avoided this situation easily as you will discover in this chapter.*

Exploration: Discovering Your Preferences for Breathing

This exploration in experiential anatomy can be performed in a chair or semi-supine on a mat (lying down on the floor with knees bent). It is useful to have a notebook nearby to record your observations as suggested periodically throughout the movement exploration.

Part 1

Take a moment to locate your lungs on the skeleton chart provided (Figure 8.1) or just visualize where your lungs are in your torso. Write down a bit about what you know about the lungs, the diaphragm, and breathing. It may be that you have some prior understand-

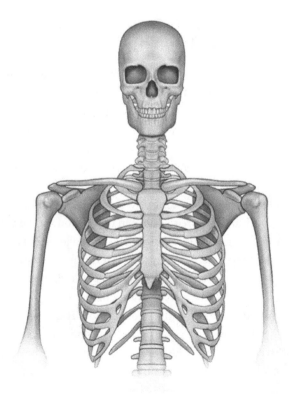

FIGURE 8.1 Rib cage. (*Source/author*: Functional Awareness® and artist Caitlin Duckwall)

ing about the breathing mechanism or you may only know that smoking is bad for the lungs. There is no judgment in what you know. It is a starting point of reference for your explorations, a baseline for your current knowledge.

Part 2

This guided movement exploration is a Romita-designed practice to improve awareness of breathing patterns. For an audio guide of this activity, see www.functionalawareness. org/.

1. Notice your breathing. Visualize where you see your breath going as it comes into the body and its journey through to exhale.
2. Notice the length of your inhalations and exhalations. You might use a counting system to give yourself a relative measure of time for both.
3. Inhale through the nose and exhale out the mouth; inhale through the mouth and exhale out the nose; inhale and exhale through the nose; or inhale and exhale through the mouth. Note how you prefer to breathe.
4. Where is the tip of your tongue resting? Where is the belly of the tongue resting? Stop and sit up and record what you have noticed thus far.

The Anatomy: Skeletal and Muscular Considerations for Breathing

Many people have a cortical map or body map with the lungs lower in the rib cage and smaller. The unconscious mismap of the lungs and misperceptions about breathing provide idiosyncratic breathing patterns and a lack of general efficiency in breathing. This inefficient breathing pattern has an effect on musicality and expressivity in dance.

The lungs begin at the first rib, just above the collarbone or clavicle, and inferiorly rest between the fourth and fifth rib (Figure 8.2). So "breathing into your belly" is not an anatomical function. It is a lovely metaphor to encourage muscular support for breathing, but it also can lead to misunderstanding. There is muscular support for breath in the lower portion of the torso, but there are no lungs in this region. In the front, or anteriorly, the ribs have greater expansion because of the costal cartilage. The true ribs (1 to 7) have the least mobility because they attach directly to the sternum. The false ribs (8 through 10) and the floating ribs (11 and 12) have greater mobility. The diaphragm drapes from the top of the dome at the fourth rib and attaches along the false ribs.

The diaphragm interdigitates with the psoas major. The psoas major is one of the muscles from Chapter 3 that provides postural support and hip flexion. The psoas originates at the twelfth thoracic vertebra where its fibers weave with those of the diaphragm. The psoas major continues along the front of the spine and attaches onto a knob on the inside of the upper thigh known as the lesser trochanter. In other words, how you stand and maintain the pelvic tilt has a profound effect on breathing. For a moment stand up

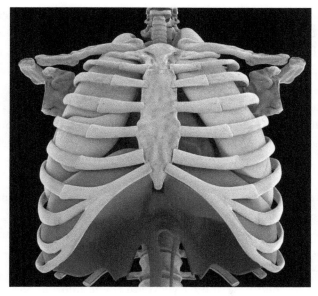

FIGURE 8.2 Location of lungs in thoracic cage. (*Source/author*: Shutterstock)

with an anterior tilt or sway back and lock your knees. Try to take a deep breath in. Now release the knees and return to a neutral pelvis and try another inhale. You might notice quite a difference in the ability to take in the air. This inability to take in air was what was happening to the middle school choral students. With knees and back tight, the psoas would not allow the diaphragm to easefully expand and contract. See the connection between these two muscles in Figure 6.2.

Exploration: Breathing Patterns

Part 1

Become acquainted with the specific breathing approach in this activity. Inhale through the nose and then exhale out the mouth, making an "sssss" or "sh" sound. Practice this several times. It will be used through the entirety of this exploration.

1. Place your hands at your lower abdomen and pelvis and allow yourself to observe the movement in the lower part of your torso using the "sss" or "sh" breathing. Do not force anything to happen. Notice if there is movement under your hands or in the lower abdomen.
2. Place your hands on your upper ribs. Do this by crossing your arms across your chest so each hand lands on the opposite side of the rib cage. Inhale through the nose, with the "sss" or "sh" sound to exhale. Notice if there is movement in this region of the body underneath your fingers. Sense the movement of the intercostal muscles

moving into three-dimensional expansion on the inhalation and releasing from expansion on the exhalation.

3. Place your hands on your collarbone and upper chest and breathe into the upper lungs or auxiliary respiratory system. Notice the movement in the cervical spine as you inhale and exhale.

4. Finally place your thumbs under your armpits and visualize breath traveling to the lungs, which are by the upper ribs. Place your hands gently around your neck and see if there is movement in the neck as you breathe. Record your discoveries.

Part 2

1. Allow for breath while thinking of the spine as a stainless steel rod from between your ears down to your tailbone. Sense how this feels.

2. Now change the image to the spine as a soft weeping willow branch and the breath is like the wind.

3. Think of the spine as seaweed and notice how this shifts your breath.

4. Finally move to child pose and let yourself breathe into the posterior portion of your lungs.

5. Record your findings.

Your Findings and Why They Matter

Discovering your habitual function for breathing allows for an increased awareness of your patterns of use. Learning some key components about the anatomical function allows you to make different choices to explore greater freedom in movement.

If you sense movement when your hands are on the ribs, your breathing preference is using more intercostal activity and less the diaphragm and psoas for action. Some people prefer to gasp air in through the mouth. This action can overuse the muscles of the neck. The spine is not a stainless steel rod, but rather a series of vertebrae and discs that allow for movement, more like a spring than a rod. On inhalation or inspiration the spine moves into a slight arching of the neck, chest, and low back. On exhalation the muscles return to the stasis of the spine. The rotatores and multifidus muscles of the transversospinalis encourage a small bit of movement between each vertebra.

Mindfulness in Dance Class

Lift the head and chest into extension (a back cambré in ballet or a suspension in contemporary dance). Notice your breath in response to this action. Many students hold their breath when arching their back, which can sometimes cause a brief dizziness or seeing stars. An inhalation can support this motion. To return the spine to upright, release the head with a slight nod of the chin as you exhale to return. Is this different than your habit?

How does awareness of your breathing patterns affect the musicality of breath? Explore this in class by performing a phrase without thinking of your breath, and then later return it with breath purposely choreographed into the phrase.

Mindfulness in Daily Life

Before you sleep, practice the three cycles of breathing to allow for a mindful enlivening of the breathing system before rest. Notice your preference for breathing when you are tired, happy, sad, or excited. Observe the changes in how you are holding your body in relation to breath. If you change your breathing, does this change your body or your mood at all?

Master dance educator and Certified Movement Analyst Peggy Hackney speaks eloquently about the breathing mechanism in her book *Making Connections* (see Further Readings):

> We breathe automatically, but breath can be influenced by and is reflective of changes in consciousness, feelings, and thoughts . . . The key element in usefulness of medical-scientific information to increase movement facility is the degree to which it facilitates a more lively moving image of physiological or neuromuscular connections within the body (pp. 51–60).

Core Support

Core support is the skeletal, muscular, and myofascial recruitment needed to maintain a balanced center of gravity (COG) in any position. Core support involves coordinated alignment and multiple muscle actions. The muscles of the "core" are not solely the superficial muscles of our abdomen, such as the "'six pack'" rectus abdominis and the obliques; the core muscles are all around the trunk—front, back, and side—and include muscles that are very deep, close to the spine. These deep muscles of the trunk include the psoas and transversospinalis group, mentioned in Chapter 3, as well as the muscles of the pelvic floor. When the balance between the feet and the head is not coordinated, the fast twitch (Type 2) mobilizing muscle fibers of the transversus abdominis, internal and external obliques, and rectus abdominis will have ineffective value in movement function. However, when the fast twitch mobilizing muscle works in concert with the transversospinalis, the diaphragm, and the action in the pelvic floor, it facilitates a dynamic synergy for efficient use of the body in action. The central musculoskeletal support system that stabilizes the trunk and also mobilizes the torso for action is referred to as central support in Functional Awareness®.

The Story: Sometimes Less Is More

A dance major was in chronic low back pain and her diagnosis was muscle strain in the low back. She attended sessions in physical therapy that aided in her recovery. Although this therapy relieved the pain for a while, the chronic back pain still recurred. In assessing her standing, a gentle hand was placed on her low back and pelvis. The dancer was holding her abdominal muscles very tightly, so tightly it was pushing her pelvis into posterior tilt. This stance, in turn, hyperextended the upper back and the weight of the thoracic spine was congregating at the low back where she reported pain. In some ways she was trying too hard to fix muscle weaknesses by gripping or overusing the superficial core musculature. A resilient body for dancing develops a balance between recruitment and release, between exertion and recuperation. Understanding abdominal support in relation to the pelvic floor and the plumb line of balance from head to feet enabled the dance major to move into a more resilient dynamic alignment and relieved her chronic pain. Efficiency in action sometimes requires the dancer to do less to achieve more.

Exploration: What Is Core or Central Support?

Consider your baseline of knowledge for core support:

1. What is your current understanding of the muscles of core support?
2. What exercises, if any, do you practice frequently to address core support?

There are many excellent programs for conditioning the body to strengthen core support. Functional Awareness˚ is not about conditioning. FA develops greater sensory and cognitive understanding for the central support in order for the conditioning practices to be more effective, and FA provides simple, mindful practices in daily tasks to help sustain the benefits from those rigorous core workouts of your choice.

In Functional Awareness˚ the investigation of anatomical function for the central or core support begins deep in the torso and then progresses to the more superficial muscular structures. The core is a series of muscular layers that work in concert to sustain the body in upright posture, aid in all motions of the trunk, and function to enable efficient lifting, swinging, and partnering. They sustain the integrity of the body in action. The deepest muscles for central support are examined in detail in Chapter 3, the transversospinalis. In carrying over the lessons from the previous chapters, it is important to consider the plumb line of balance to engage core spinal support from the rotatores, multifidus, and semispinalis group on the posterior trunk while the psoas provides deep postural support on the anterior portion of the trunk. Another group of deep support muscles, at the base of the pelvis, are the muscles of the pelvic floor.

The Anatomy: Pelvic Floor

The pelvic floor refers to the muscular structure that spans across the inferior portion of the pelvis from the pubic bone to the coccyx, from ilium to coccyx, and connects the pelvis to the legs from the sacrum to the greater trochanter on the femur, and from the ischial bones to the greater trochanter.

These muscles, seen in the Figure 9.1, form a supportive hammock for the skeletal pelvic bowl. It is important to maintain an elasticity and resiliency in the pelvic floor muscles for several reasons. These muscles control urinary function, so they therefore maintain urinary track health. The pelvic floor muscles enhance sexual satisfaction as the muscles in orgasm. The pelvic floor also provides a hammock of muscular support for the internal organs in the lower abdomen.

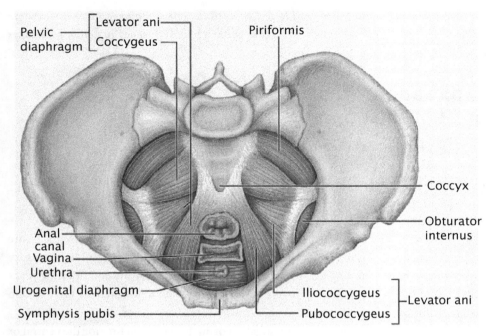

FIGURE 9.1 Muscles of the pelvic floor. (*Source/author*: Shutterstock)

The levator ani, coccygeus, piriformis, and obturator muscles of the pelvic floor are important for dancers because they coordinate with breath to support action to move the pelvis during standing in parallel or turned out, traveling forward in space, and changing directions. The muscles of the pelvic floor are an internal steering mechanism for propelling the body.

Exploration: Sensing the Muscles of the Pelvic Floor

The muscles of the pelvic floor aid in stabilizing dancers in movement. They also regulate the flow of urine out of the body. To begin to feel these muscles and how they work, try this the next time you use the bathroom to urinate.

1. Begin the flow of urine.
2. Stop and hold the flow for a couple of seconds.
3. Let the flow begin again.
4. Repeat this several times.

You are activating the muscles of the pelvic floor. Discover these muscles while in dance class. Try activating these muscles during the day or in dance class. Explore an easy support from these muscles. Do not over-contract. Recruit the muscles for action, but do not grip. Remember it is the natural recruit and then release of muscle fiber that allow for maximum resiliency for dancing.

Your Findings and Why They Matter

For some this activity allows you to sense the pelvic floor for the first time. This is important for the health reasons described earlier. For others this activity may help refine their understanding of the pelvic floor in a kinesthetic manner, and you can use this muscle function to support the standing leg in balance or aid in propelling the pelvis through space.

The Anatomy: The Psoas Major

The psoas major is another deep muscular component of central support. As discussed previously, the psoas is a deep muscle that supports the stability of the spine and provides resiliency in pelvic movement. As you look at Figure 9.2, you can see that the fibers of the

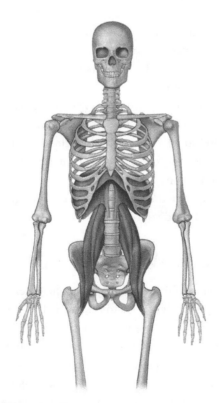

FIGURE 9.2 Psoas major and the diaphragm. (*Source/author*: Functional Awareness® and artist Caitlin Duckwall)

psoas major lie in the sides of the pelvic bowl and merge with the iliacus, connecting the trunk to the legs through the iliopsoas tendon. If this muscle is overly tight and unable to engage in both recruitment and release, your abdominal exercises will demonstrate unsatisfactory results. It is hard to touch this muscle because it rests behind the internal organs of the lower body. One can sense the changes in the body when the psoas releases.

Exploration: Releasing the Psoas Major from Habitual Contraction

1. Stand easily and move through a few développés in parallel. Notice the ease or discomfort as the hip flexes to bring the knee and foot into position.
2. Move to the floor lying on your back in semi-supine. Take a moment to allow the body to rest into the floor, letting the body yield to gravity. Let your jaw release away from your upper teeth.
3. Place a rolled up towel transversely where the sacrum meets the lumbar spine. This maintains your natural lumbar curves while lying down.
4. Take a few minutes to rest here, noticing your breathing and asking yourself to let go of any unnecessary tension. Allow three cycles of breathing in and out using the "sss" or "sh" sound from Chapter 8 to slow down the exhale.
5. Slowly extend your right knee to straighten the leg along the floor. Easily slide the leg back to a semi-supine position. This movement is inspired by the Bartenieff Fundamental Pre-thigh Lift. Repeat this action one more time on the right.
6. Extend your left knee to straighten the leg. Easily slide the leg back to a semi-supine position. Repeat this action again on the left.
7. Gently remove the towel, and let the low back begin to rest into contact with the floor.
8. Roll gently onto one side in a fetal position. Bring awareness to your breathing for several cycles of inspiration and expiration.
9. Slowly move to standing. Try the retiré and développé again and see if there is any difference in sensation. Record your findings mentally or on paper.

Your Findings and Why They Matter

Releasing the habitual tension of the psoas major can heighten a more dynamic connection from the feet through the pelvic floor to the head. This muscle, as seen in previous chapters, has several key roles in movement function. It supports the body in upright posture, it is a primary hip flexor, and it interdigitates with the fibers of the diaphragm to support breathing. Therefore the psoas is a pivotal muscle for central support. This exploration with the towel releases the tension in the psoas major to create more resiliency and ease in action. It is another way to move out of habit, allowing for greater choice in movement.

The Anatomy: Transversus Abdominis

The transversus abdominis encircles the torso from the back near the lumbar spine (at the thoracocolumbar fasciae and costal bones seven to twelve), and wraps around to the front of the body and attaches along the whole front of the torso, from the inferior tip of the breastbone, called the xiphoid process, along the strong tendon sheath of the linea alba to the pubic bone. The transversus abdominis creates a girdle to support the torso from ribs to hips. It also has fibers that interconnect with the diaphragm. If you do not engage the transversus abdominis effectively, your stability in the lower back and pelvis is compromised.

Superficial to the transversus abdominis are the internal and external obliques. These muscles support side bending and spiral movements of the trunk. The diagonal fibers of the internal and external obliques aid in twisting and contribute to central support. Alongside the transversus abdominis in Figure 9.3 is the most superficial abdominal muscle, the rectus abdominis. This muscle originates at the xiphoid process of the sternum and travels along the front of the abdomen to the pubic bone. It is often referred to as the six-pack muscle. Together these muscles are the primary mobilizers of the torso, capable of supporting the body in wonderful actions that require strength and agility.

Exploration: Discovering Your Transversus Abdominis

1. The transversus abdominis is one of the primary muscles you can feel when you cough. Place your hand on your belly and cough a few times. You will feel a muscle

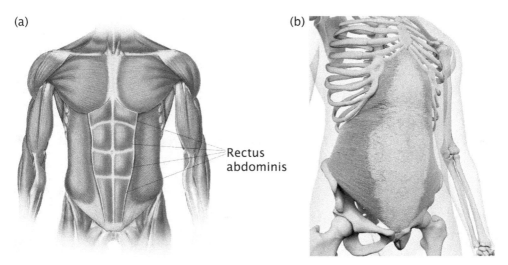

(a)

(b)

Rectus abdominis

FIGURE 9.3 (a) Rectus abdominis (*Source/author*: Functional Awareness® and artist Caitlin Duckwall) (b) tranversus abdominis. (*Source/author*: Shutterstock)

pulling in. This is the tranversus abdominis aiding the diaphragm to help expel forced air from your lungs. If you hold it too tightly, it inhibits breathing.

2. Perform any abdominal series of your choosing. Exhale on the action that requires the flexion of the trunk. Add an audible "haa" sound for each exhalation to expel the air more forcibly. This sound ensures engagement of the transversus abdominis in action.

Exploration: Discovering Your Rectus Abdominis

The rectus abdominis is the muscle that is engaged when you do a standard "crunch." This is a good exercise to feel the concentric contraction of this muscle. The following exploration investigates the eccentric action of the rectus abdominis.

1. Begin in semi-supine. Reach your arms over your head and sit up in one count.
2. With arms extended forward begin to release your chin to the chest and roll down to the floor in eight slow counts, keeping the knees bent and the feet completely on the floor. Think about each vertebra connecting sequentially to the floor as you lower in these eight slow counts.
3. Make note if you skip some sections of the spine as you roll down. This may indicate where your back is tight or less flexible and your front or anterior trunk is less stable.
4. Repeat Steps 1 through 4 several times.

These abdominal exercises also strengthen the more superficial rectus abdominis to ensure greater stability for the back and torso when lifting, carrying, or supporting your own weight during floor work. Plank and side plank are also excellent exercises to engage the central support system and develop greater stability through the center/core of the body.

Your Findings and Why They Matter

Your breathing is inextricably linked to the central or core neuromuscular and myofascial support systems. Holding the belly in too tightly can restrict breathing and impose restrictions on your ability to have a strong central support system for dancing.

Mindfulness in Dance Class

1. Let the anatomical imagery of the pelvic floor and your experience to engage these muscles buoy you during an exercise or phrase in class. See how this changes your experience with the movement. Does it also change stability or phrasing?

2. If asked to pull up in your belly during a standing exercise in dance class, support the transversus abdominis at 30 percent of its contraction ability. Save the greater contraction of the transversus abdominis muscle for movements that require strength. Constant over-engagement restricts action and expressivity instead of enhancing your skill.

Mindfulness in Daily Life

Think of a supportive hammock of the pelvic floor supporting your pelvis finding balance when you're going about your day—no need to suck in, just think of the pelvis moving up.

Expressivity of Arms

The arm structure has complex skeletal features, joint articulations, and many muscular attachments to the trunk. This structure enables a wide variety of expressive movements for the arms. Gesture is an intricate element of artistic expression in dance. Inadvertently a dancer can restrict their possible full range of movement for gesture. Dancers can have a tendency to have their shoulders rolled forward in the glenohumeral joint or shoulder socket. This restricts free and easy range of motion of the arms.

The Story: To Sleep, Perchance to Dream

Jennifer mentioned during dance technique class that she was experiencing restricted move-ment in her shoulder. She was finding it more and more difficult to raise her arm overhead for any movements in class. Physical therapy, specific exercises, and taping the shoulder proved useful, but the issue was not fully resolving. I asked Jennifer about her daily activities, and then asked her about her sleep position. Jennifer explained that she slept on her side in a fetal position. She did not sleep on the side with her restricted shoulder pressing into the bed. This was helpful because she was not adding additional pressure to the shoulder while sleeping; however, she was hanging her shoulder forward in an unsupported manner and placing strain on the tendons and ligaments (see Figure 10.1).

Often it is not the rigorous activity of dance causing muscular imbalance; it is in dance class that the symptom or restriction becomes more apparent. We sleep for six to nine hours nightly. Certain sleep postures can create imbalances in the neuromuscular and myofascial systems. For Jennifer, sleeping on one side exacerbated the imbalance in the shoulder and arm structure. A supportive pillow to prevent the shoulder from rolling forward during the night reinforced the balance she was working to maintain. This simple prop of the pillow sup-ported her sleep cycle and her arm structure to assist in regaining full range of motion. Func-tional Awareness® is a series of kinesthetic tools for listening and sensing the body during dance class and outside of dance class . . . even in sleep!

FIGURE 10.1 Sleep position. (*Source/author*: With permission from Jim Burger Photography)

Exploration: Axial Integrity to Support Appendicular Action of the Arms

1. Sit in a slump or C-curve, resting on your sacrum and sense your shoulders curl in response to this.
2. Bring your arms to first position with the fingertips about the height of your belly button.
3. Attempt to bring your arms overhead into fifth position. What do you notice?
4. Now undo the slump, allow for a breath, and move into an easeful yet long spine. Think of a warm sun at the center of the chest and let the sunbeams radiate from that central point all the way out to the fingertips. Repeat the movement of arms from first to fifth position overhead. How does coming to upright balance in sitting affect the ease of movement in the arms?
5. Try this same activity when standing.

Your Findings and Why They Matter

Curling into fetal or sitting in a C-curve is a useful capability and necessary in some forms of dance expression (e.g., contraction). This action involves elevation and forward tilt of the scapula and the ball of the humerus rotates anteriorly forward in the glenohumeral joint. When we leave dance class to go to school, work, or rest at home in front of the computer or TV, we can unwittingly spend hours in this slump, which reinforces a restriction in the expressivity and range of motion of the arms. The ability to shift, change, choose, and adapt is the key to resiliency and discovering your full movement potential.

The Anatomy: Biomechanical Distinctions of the Glenohumeral Joint and Scapula

The arm structure is part of the appendicular skeleton and is comprised of the clavicle, scapula, humerus, radius, and ulna. The arm structure skeletally attaches to the axial skeleton at one point, where the clavicle meets the sternum portion of the rib cage: the sternoclavicular joint. The acromioclavicular joint is at the top of the shoulder where the scapula meets the clavicle (Figure 10.2, A and B). The glenohumeral joint, where the head of the humerus meets the glenoid fossa, is commonly referred to as the shoulder joint.

Muscular Support for Arms

The primary muscles supporting the glenohumeral joint are the four muscles of the rotator cuff, the supraspinatus, infraspinatus, teres minor, and subscapularus (Figure 10.3). Each of these muscles connects the glenohumeral ball-and-socket joint to the rest of the

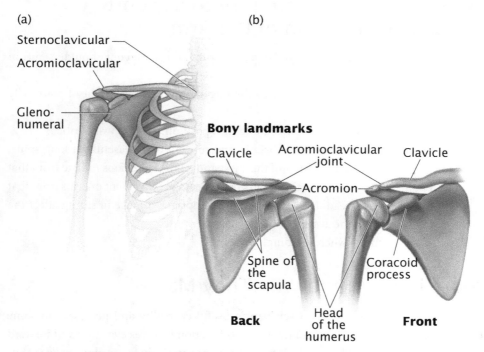

FIGURE 10.2 Skeletal landmarks of the upper arm structure. (*Source/author*: Functional Awareness® and artist Caitlin Duckwall)

Rotator Cuff Muscles

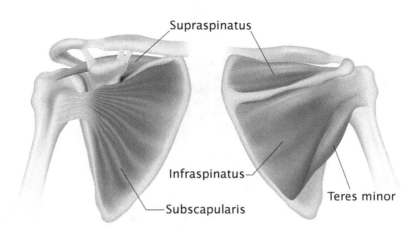

Supraspinatus

Infraspinatus

Subscapularis

Teres minor

Anterior view   Posterior view

FIGURE 10.3 Muscles of the rotator cuff. (*Source/author*: Shutterstock)

torso and supports its full range of action. The latissimus dorsi, the trapezius muscles on the posterior torso, and the pectoralis major on the front are large superficial muscles that stabilize the trunk (Figure 10.4). The latissimus spans the wide swath of the back and then spirals to insert onto the front of the upper arm at the upper third of the bicipital ridge. The pectoralis major spans across the front of the chest from the sternum and also attaches to the upper third of the bicipital ridge of the humerus.

Exploration: The Eight Motions of the Scapula

1. This exploration can be performed on your own trying Steps a through h, 2 and 3. The activity may also be performed with partners. In pairs, Partner A stands in front of Partner B. Partner B places his or her hands on the scapula of Partner A. This placement will provide a tactile sensory experience of the gliding movement that the scapula performs to support arm and shoulder movement.
   a. Elevation: Lift the shoulder blades up toward your ears.
   b. Depression: Press the shoulder blades back down along the ribs.
   c. Adduction (retraction): Pull the shoulder blades in toward the spine.
   d. Abduction (protraction): Move the shoulder blades away from the spine.
   e. Upward rotation: The natural swing of the inferior tip of the scapula is to swing away from the spine and upward. Bring the fingertips from touching the side seams of the pants and move the arms out in front to first position and then

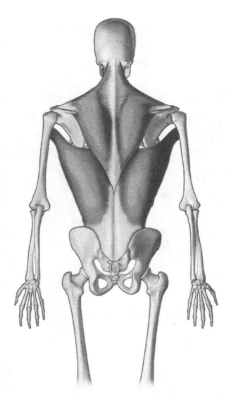

FIGURE 10.4 Latissimus dorsi and trapezius. (*Source/author*: Functional Awareness® and artist Caitlin Duckwall)

       overhead to fifth; you can sense this gliding motion of the inferior scapula gliding slightly up and out.

  f. Downward rotation: The inferior tip of the scapula swings toward the spine and down, which you can sense as you return your arms to your side.

  g. Forward tilt: Once the shoulders elevate a small bit, the scapula can move forward to create the sensation often referred to as hunching.

  h. Return from forward tilt: You can release from the hunching forward position to neutral scapula and this movement is called return from forward tilt.

2. Lift the scapula into elevation quickly. Notice what the neck and head do in relation to this movement. Do you ever experience your shoulders lifting unintentionally while dancing? If this occurs, pause for a moment and allow for a breath to let the scapula release into a rested place on the posterior ribs.

3. Partner B places her hands on the Partner A's scapula as Partner A walks forward. Partner B walks along forward with them, keeping the hands lightly on the shoulder blades. Notice the easy "leaf on the stream" motion of the scapula with the easy swing of the arm structure as Partner A walks.

4. Change positions with your partner.

Exploration: Movements of the Glenohumeral Joint

1. Stand in a comfortable parallel and consider the tripod of balance of the feet and the easeful balance at the AO joint at the top of the spine. Continue standing and move your glenohumeral joint through the following actions.

   a. Flexion: Think of the thumbs leading the action and swing the arm forward.
      i. Do your head and neck want to swing forward as well?
      ii. Move toward ease through the axial skeleton. Think of the wide pectoralis major and latissimus stabilizing the trunk so just the arm structure moves. Allow the head and neck to remain balanced over the spine as the arm moves forward.
   b. Extension: Swing the arm directly behind you. How does your spine react to this action?
   c. Abduction: Bring both arms out to the side up to shoulder height.
   d. Adduction: Let the arms move back down and then cross in front of the body, so your wrists cross.
   e. Medial rotation: Place your left hand on the right upper arm, near the head of the humerus and gently turn the whole arm inward toward the body.
   f. Lateral rotation: Let the left hand remain on the head of the right humerus and gently turn the whole arm outward away from the body.
      i. Move the left hand to the right scapula by touching the tip with the back of your hand or have a partner feel it. Does it move if you turn the arm inward and outward? It should move because the scapula's muscle support attaches to the upper arm.
      ii. Now try to press the shoulder blades down and hold them in place as you move the arm. This movement actually restricts easeful action in the arm.
   g. Circumduction: Move the arm in a large circle, swinging front overhead and then come to the back to complete the circle.

Your Findings and Why They Matter

The scapula is like a leaf on a stream. It glides and moves through the eight motions in response to the actions of the spine, shoulder, and breath. It is not fixed and it can restrict motion if we think we have to force the shoulder blades down the back and secure the scapula with tension. As discovered in Chapter 9 on core support, over-contraction of a muscle group can restrict action and ease in movement rather than support the body.

Exploration: Moving the Arms through a Dance Phrase

1. Choose a familiar sequence of arm movements practiced in dance class.
2. As you begin the phrase with your arms, notice whether your scapula and shoulders have a tendency to elevate or lift toward your ears.
3. Take a moment to envision the large latissimus beginning at the sacrum and fanning out and spiraling around to insert to the front of your upper arm. It is like a broad mainsail of a ship supporting you where you want to navigate the arms for expression.
4. Repeat this same arm phrase from above in two more ways. First lead all the arm movement distally through your fingertips. Next repeat it by leading all the movement from a mid-proximal location, letting the shoulder joint lead all the movement. What do you notice?

Your Findings and Why They Matter

Dancing is a lifelong exploration to discover the balance of the necessary recruitment needed for a movement with the least amount of strain to the system. Discovering the balanced support of the superficial latissimus dorsi and pectoralis major to sustain expressive use of the arm structure is a process of opening through your front without sheering the ribs forward and supporting through the back without pinching the shoulder blades in and down. Whether you lead with the fingertips or move from your shoulder joints, let the shoulder blade glide into action easily with deep central support and see how this affects your dancing.

Mindfulness in Dance Class

There are often four to eight musical counts before each dance exercise as an introduction to the tempo. During the introduction, consider the tripod of balance at the feet, the balance at the AO joint, and the muscular support of the latissimus dorsi and pectoralis major. See if the anatomical images for balance for length and width support the carriage of the arms.

Mindfulness in Daily Life

1. Notice your overall posture when sitting at the computer or in class. If you are in a C-curve, can you feel the glenohumeral joint rolled forward? Is the scapula in elevation or forward tilt? Decide whether this is a useful place to be for the particular activity that you are doing. Is it habit or is it choice?

2. When reaching for something on a shelf, such as a coffee mug, or raising an arm to ask a question, notice where you like to initiate this movement. Try different approaches to the same action of the arms.

3. Notice your arm structure in relation to your sleep position. Does your sleep position support a balanced arm structure? Try using different comfortable alternatives.

Recuperation and Restoring Balance

There are many approaches to mindful practice that elicit recuperation of the body–mind system. Dance requires a great deal of physical exertion and the body often holds tension needed for dancing long after class or rehearsal is over. Time for recuperation and restoration is an important part of any physical activity. A major aspect of rest is sleep! Arranging and then implementing a regular sleep cycle can support a healthy immune system and aid the body in restoring the micro tearing of muscle tissue that is a natural part of building a strong and resilient dancer. The body needs time to repair muscles, regain strength, and replenish energy through sleep. A regular and sufficient sleep pattern should be a priority for all humans, especially for dancers.

This chapter provides three practices for recuperation through imagery and gentle guided movements. These recuperation explorations are helpful to release tension and restore balance. You may also be guided through the explorations by listening to the audio files (www.functionalawareness.org). In addition to the three explorations below, the sequence of mindfulness in breathing in Chapter 9 is a beneficial practice to release tension and return to balance. You may move through these explorations in a chair if lying down on your back with your knees bent in a semi-supine position is not comfortable.

Recuperation Practice 1: A Practice in Neurological Inhibition to Release Tension

Part 1: Right Side

1. Begin by lying down on the floor. Lie down with legs extended and arms extended, by your side, with the palms facing up.

2. Let your body release into the floor. Yield to gravity. Allow the weight of the heels to sense the contact with the earth. Let the weight of the head be taken by the floor. Let your jaw release away from your upper teeth. Bring an easy attention to your breathing.

3. Notice your right leg from the hip to the tips of the toes. Contract the muscles in the right leg and hold on to this contraction. As you are contracting the right leg, notice your lower back. Did it also tense up? Think of releasing the unnecessary tension. Notice your shoulders. Are they tensing to help your legs contract? Think of letting go in the shoulders while continuing to tense the right leg.

4. Release the tension in the right leg now. Gently move the leg around in the hip socket and let go of the contraction.

5. Notice if there is a difference between the right leg that you have just used in contraction and the other leg. Often there is a change in sensation between the two legs, demonstrating a shift in resting length in the muscle spindle that determines the level of tension needed for body action.

6. Make a fist and tense the muscles of the entire right arm from shoulder to fingers. Hold this pose. Notice your neck and see if it is holding tension. Ask yourself to let your neck release. Notice if your jaw has tightened and allow the lower teeth to release away from the upper teeth. Let your breathing support greater ease as you continue to contract the right arm.

7. Open the hand gently and release the tension in the arm. Move the arm in any easy pathway to help release the tension required in the contraction activity.

8. Observe if there is a difference between the right arm and the left.

9. You have now contracted the right arm and right leg. Do you sense any difference between the right and left sides of the body? You probably have discovered some patterns where the body creates tension in your shoulders or jaw, or where you hold your breath or tighten your stomach, no matter what part of the body is asked to contract. These unnecessary tensions deplete energy and contribute to inefficiency in action. As you begin the sequence on the left side, the instructions will ask you to undo unnecessary tension before you begin contracting the body part.

Part 2: Left Side

10. Notice your left leg from the hip to the tips of the toes.

11. This time, before contracting the muscles in the left leg, ask yourself to pause and allow for a breath. Release unwanted tension from the extraneous body parts as you contract the muscles of the left leg. Hold the left leg firmly tense as you continue easy breathing, asking yourself to continue to let go of unnecessary tension.

12. Release the contraction in the left leg now. Gently move the leg around a bit.

13. Notice how both legs feel and gently bend one knee and then the other to bring the feet to the floor into the semi-supine position.

14. Before you make a fist and tense the muscles of the entire left arm, notice your neck and see if it is holding tension. Ask yourself to let the neck release. Notice if your jaw

has tightened and allow the lower teeth to release away from the upper teeth. Notice your breathing and then make the fist with the left hand and contract the muscles in the left arm. Can you sense that you are doing the required action with less overall tension in the body?

15. Open the hand gently and release the tension in the arm. Gently move the arm in an easy pathway to help release the tension. It is a bit like the game of patting your head and rubbing your stomach. In practicing this brain game and inhibiting your habitual responses to do simple actions, the body teaches itself to let go of unwanted tension.

16. Bring both shoulders up by your ears and hold them there. Continue to hold them up as you check in with your breathing. Ask yourself, "Where can I do less, and still hold my shoulders up?" It is a playful exploration.

17. Now release both shoulders down and come to a place of ease in the whole body.

18. Notice general tension level within. Did this change from the beginning of the exploration?

Your Findings and Why They Matter

Recuperation Practice 1 invites you to contract, tense, and hold certain parts of the body for 5 to 10 seconds and then release this tension, enabling the muscles to shift the relaxed resting length of the muscle fibers. The guided practice above heightens awareness of unnecessary tension and invites the body to release this unwarranted muscle contraction.

Mindfulness in Dance Class

After dance class or between dance class and rehearsal, take a moment to recuperate in a semi-supine position. Explore tensing and releasing body parts to activate awareness and sense where you can let go of unnecessary tension.

Mindfulness in Daily Life

When you are a passenger in a car or on public transportation, simply move through the above exploration and practice letting go in other body parts to reduce unnecessary tension. Remember to let the breath support you in the exploration. Recuperation Practice 1 is especially useful when flying on airplanes. It provides a release in tension and allows the body to move without disturbing the folks around you.

Recuperation Practice 2: Rebalancing the Hips, Legs, and Feet

1. Begin in a semi-supine position. Take a moment to release into the floor. Yield to gravity. Notice the weight of the feet and where they make contact with the floor. Notice your breathing without judgment or expectation. Notice inspiration as the air spills in and ask yourself to consider letting go of unnecessary tension on the exhalation.

2. Observe the soles of your feet and how they find contact with the floor. In terms of tripod of balance, are you easily balanced on all three points or do the feet have a different balance at this moment? Do not immediately change; just nonjudgmentally notice how you unconsciously balance the leg.

3. Reconsider the tripod of balance in both feet.

4. Gently extend the right knee and slide the leg straight out along the floor. As you slide, be mindful of maintaining the tripod of balance. Maintain the leg in parallel even after it is completely straight. The body will have a natural tendency to let the leg laterally rotate or turnout.

5. Pause for a moment. Allow for breath. Ask yourself if there are any places in your body where you can let go of any unnecessary tension.

6. Draw the leg into flexion by sliding the foot along the floor. As the leg moves from straight out to bent knee position find the tripod of the foot on the floor. Notice if you favor the outside or inside through inversion or eversion of the foot during this process. Give additional attention to the distal head of the first metatarsal. Observe if this shifts your pathway into a new habit for bending the knee.

7. As you rest the foot back onto the floor with the knee bent, be mindful of the tripod of balance and let all three points of contact have equal weight into the floor.

8. Repeat this sliding out and bending the knee pattern 3 times. This allows for neural repatterning in the body.

9. Repeat this process on the other leg.

Finish the sequence with both knees bent. Let yourself make small adjustments in the body to allow for length in the spine to support the changes in the legs.

Your Findings and Why They Matter

It is common for dancers to have overdeveloped thigh muscles on the more lateral side of the leg and less strength toward the inner thighs. This situation can create an imbalance at the knee and lower leg because there is greater torque on the hinge joint. This quiet restorative process gently brings awareness to habit and creates new patterning for bending and straightening the leg.

Mindfulness in Dance Class

Recuperation Practice 2 aids to restore balance in the musculature of the legs after the rigorous demands of dance class. It is restful and an alternative to foam rolling as an approach to release thigh tension before or following dance class.

Mindfulness in Daily Life

When you are sitting in a chair, notice your habitual positions for the feet and legs. There is no judgment in this activity, just an opportunity to become aware of how your feet and legs prefer to support you while sitting. Consider repositioning the feet through the tripod of balance to recuperate from any asymmetrical patterns you notice.

Recuperation Practice 3: Releasing Tension in the Arms (Snow Angel)

1. Begin on the floor in a semi-supine position. Rest with arms extended with the palms facing up.
2. Notice your breathing. Notice inspiration as the air spills in and ask yourself to consider letting go of unnecessary tension on the exhalation.
3. Let the lips remain together as the teeth rest slightly apart to release unnecessary tension in the temporomandibular joint.
4. Think of an image of water spilling from your neck, down both arms, and all the way through your fingertips.
5. Now give the water a color. In the instructions that follow, think of the color like finger paint, and let your fingers lead the actions of the arms. This movement is called distal initiation of the arm.
6. With the palms facing up, move both arms away from your hips toward your head. At first move both arms like a butterfly opening its wings. Move just 2 or 3 inches and rest.
7. Flip the hands to face down, slowly leading with the fingertips, and rest again.
8. Let the fingertips lead the action; turn the palms to face up again and travel several more inches, opening the butterfly wings so the arms are outstretched forming a T-shape with the body.
9. Flip the hands to face down slowly and rest.
10. Flip the palms to face up again and travel several more inches so the arms form a high V-shape above shoulder height. Let your butterfly wings fully open.
11. Pause to allow for mindfulness of a few cycles of breath, and let your jaw release away from the upper teeth.
12. Return to close the butterfly wings. When moving the arms back down toward your thighs, the hands are facing palms down during the descent.
13. With the fingertips leading the action distally, travel to lower the arms to the T-shape and then pause and flip the palms up.
14. Turn the hands one last time to face down and make your descent to close the butterfly wings and rest the arms by your side.
15. Turn the palms up to finish the movement.
16. Pause and rest to allow for a moment to release unwanted tension.

Your Findings and Why They Matter

It is not unusual for dancers to experience tension in the shoulders, neck, and jaw. This activity has the nickname of the snow angel because if feels like a slower, mindful version of that activity we perform when falling on our backs in the snow. It should also have that childlike sense of play and fun. The activity naturally engages the muscles of the rotator cuff while allowing the body to release from tension that is often the residue of habitual action. Let yourself enjoy the movement.

Mindfulness in Dance Class

Recuperation Practice 3 can be done standing along a wall or lying down on the floor before class to open the arm structure and release tension to enhance expressivity of the arms during class.

Mindfulness in Daily Life

When going to reach for something on a shelf, such as a coffee mug, or to raise an arm to ask a question, notice where you like to initiate this movement. Play with different approaches to the same action of the arms. Initiate it distally from your fingertips. Initiate it more proximally from your shoulders first. Explore the differences.

Conclusion

Gathering the Knowledge to Move Forward

The previous chapters offer a series of movement explorations that engage the readers in anatomical body mapping and encourage them to experiment, explore, and discover things about their own body and their habitual choices in movement. The beauty of artistic expression is within the myriad of ways humans are capable of moving and communicating through movement and dance. Functional Awareness® investigates the ways in which dancers can embody their artistry and expression while maintaining a healthy body. It is important for the body to release unnecessary tension as it often impedes performance and can cause pain. Once released, the mover has the ability to recruit the required muscles for dynamic alignment. It is essential to recuperate; this can be done through moving toward balance. Through anecdotal stories and anatomical explanations of the body, the reader learns that no one is symmetrical or perfectly balanced. Yet everyone has the ability to make changes and move with ease.

At the closing of each Functional Awareness® workshop or course, we have a final practice at the end of each session called 'beach glass and shells.' It is a time to gather thoughts of what you have experienced.

The Story: *Beach Glass and Shells*

Both authors have spent countless hours together on the beaches of New York, Florida, Delaware, and Maryland. When walking along the beach we might focus our eyes out onto the horizon. Then we gaze along the beach. We scan for objects resting in the sand. We become curious about a shell or horseshoe crab. Occasionally there is something that captivates our attention and engages us enough to pick it up, spend more time with it, and put it in our pocket as a keepsake to remember the day or the moment. Perhaps it is a glimmering piece of smooth sea-foam-colored beach glass; or perhaps it is an unusually shaped shell. Pick it up, put in the pocket, and save it to examine further at another time or leave it in the pocket to just feel later in the day and remember.

During your journey of reading the book, what discoveries or ideas engaged you? What questions or further inquiries bubbled up during the course of chapters? What are

FIGURE 12.1 Beach Glass and Shells (*Source/author*: With permission from Jim Burger Photography)

those morsels of information or experiences that you've picked up along the way? What are your shells or pieces of beach glass?

Writing Exploration: Beach Glass and Shells

1. What concepts during the readings call for further play and exploration?
    a. Take a moment to reflect on what concepts, imagery, or movement explorations might be a piece of beach glass for you.
    b. Glance back through the book and find one thing in each chapter to record as your beach glass or shell.
        i.   It can be something you question and wish to investigate further.
        ii. It can be something that engaged you and you want to put into practice.

Further Steps: Putting It into Practice

Continue to bring awareness to your habitual patterns of movement and how they affect your dancing and your everyday life. Continue to seek the end-ranges of movement and explore the reaches of your artistry. Enjoy the energetic satisfaction of exertion and also allow time for recuperation. Recuperation can be as simple as a moment's pause, to allow for breath to release, recruit, and recover. Balance can be a moment's consideration of the tripod at the feet to move toward balance in the body. We invite you to utilize Functional Awareness®: Anatomy in Action and the shells and beach glass you've collected thus far as tools for discovery, exploration, and change.

Glossary of Terms in Human Anatomy

PLANES OF THE BODY

transverse or horizontal: plane divides the body into upper and lower parts, superior and inferior.
median or mid-sagittal: plane divides the body in right and left halves
coronal or frontal: plane divides the body into front and back, or anterior and posterior parts.

ANATOMICAL TERMS OF REFERENCE

anterior: indicates the front of the body.
posterior: indicates the back portion of the body.
superior: indicates a position on the body above the point of reference.
inferior: indicates a position on the body below the point of reference.
proximal: indicates closer to the trunk, or joint of reference.
distal: indicates farther from the trunk or joint of reference.
flexion: indicates movement in the sagittal plane that takes the body forward.
extension: indicates movement in the sagittal plane that takes the body backward.
ipsilateral: indicates movement on the same side of the body.
contralateral: indicates movement on opposite sides of the body.
abduction: indicates movement away from the median plane.
adduction: indicates movement towards the median plane
medial rotation: indicates movement in transverse plane moving inward.
lateral rotation: indicates movement in the transverse (horizontal) plane moving outward.
superficial: designates position on the exterior part of the body.
deep: designates a position on an internal part of the body.
supination: indicates movement with the palm of the hand facing forward (as if it could hold a bowl of soup).
pronation: indicates a movement with the palm of the hand facing backward.